Good Times Never Seemed So Good

By Stephen Collins

Enjoy!

Good Times Never Seemed So Good by Stephen Collins

© 2018 Stephen Collins

Cover design and illustrations by the author

ISBN: 9781726771597

Contents

For Sam and Joel

"Then spring became the summer…"

Neil Diamond, *Sweet Caroline*

PROLOGUE

Trying to prop the clumsy old bike up with my standing leg, I squeezed some more blood out of the gaping hole in my right knee. Get the muck out of her, Steve. I might have finished medical school just a few days earlier, but I wasn't expecting to play doctor this soon. Especially not on myself.

After being thrown from my saddle, two things had catapulted out of the front pannier bag across the road. My passport and my emergency toilet roll. I honestly couldn't have told you at that moment which I felt was more important to rescue. I wasn't going to need the passport again for a while, and you never know when an unsuspecting bidet is going to stare you in the face on the continent.

The rain was hammering down to an almost comical degree, and I was hopelessly lost. Cherbourg was still only fifteen miles behind me, so it would have been very, very easy to freewheel back towards the port and make arrangements for the next ferry back to Ireland. It definitely crossed my mind. The crash had left my bike's wheel alignment all over the shop, the brakes were mangled, the chain was hanging limply into a puddle and it felt like my kneecap had been smashed into fifteen thousand pieces by the pavement.

Before this tumble I'd already accidentally, illegally, spent half an hour on the French motorway with lorries screaming past at over 100 kilometres per hour, blaring their horns in my direction. To begin with, I genuinely thought this was their way of saying 'Bonjour'. What an amazingly welcoming bunch of lads the French are, I thought. Even their truckers go out of their way to offer enthusiastic greetings to visitors. After a few minutes, these horns were accompanied by ear-splitting outbursts of colourful words I'd never come across in GCSE French at school. Turned out they weren't saying "Keep up the fantastic work big fella" after all.

The blood was still streaming down my shin, and the cheap plasters refused to stick in the driving rain. I staggered in the direction of what looked like a corner shop, only to discover that all shops in this particular town closed each day between 12 noon and 2pm. Reaching for the phone in my back pocket, I took a quick glance and the soggy screen told me it was ten past twelve. Great.

What was I even doing here anyway? Just give up. Turn around, climb back onto the boat, and enjoy your hard-earned summer holidays. The further you cycle, the more difficult it is to get back home. Nobody would mind. Hardly anyone knew about my cycling plans anyway. The fundraising only had a couple of hundred quid in the kitty, so there'd be no difficulty handing that back with a quick note of apology. Just go home, I kept saying to myself. I didn't need this hassle.

By this stage I'd hauled my bike onto the damp pavement, when a concerned voice piped up behind me. "Ça va?" A blonde-haired lady leaned out of her car window into the rain, holding up a line of traffic behind her. This was my way out. My guardian angel had arrived. I saw her two children playing in the warmth of the back seat, watching cartoons on the back of their mum's headrest. We never had any of that when I was their age. Lucky rats. Probably never needed to play 'I Spy' in their lives.

I wanted to plead for help. My knee was in agony. To make matters worse, I hadn't spoken French for over ten years, and the only response I'd ever learnt to her question was "Ça va bien". So I shrugged my shoulders and that's what I said. She didn't look like she believed me one bit, but waved and carried on. I'd have given every single Euro in my bank balance to hop into that car and watch some French cartoons. And I'd have happily left my useless bike by the roadside too.

Trudging towards a spot of shelter in an alleyway, I let out an audible sigh. This is a joke. This whole cycling around France thing is such a daft idea. I desperately wanted to prove all those friends wrong who'd laughed when I first suggested my plans to them. But maybe they were right. I'm not a top athlete. I'm just a regular bloke who's far too prone to conjuring up ideas that I'm probably not capable of seeing through. I took the weather-beaten passport out of my back pocket and opened the front pannier where I kept my valuables all in one place. It was then that I saw the envelope.

Inside were tickets for each Northern Ireland game at Euro 2016, including the opening match in Nice twelve days later. I'd waited to see our country play on the big stage since I was a boy. To be honest, I'd struggled to think about anything else for the past year or so – reading countless newspaper articles, maintaining a daily ritual of checking on Kyle Lafferty's groin injury, re-watching footage of goals from our qualifying campaign grinning ear to ear, and putting university finals at risk due to the number of messages I was sending to mates back home about whether or not a 3-5-2 formation really suited the players in our squad. I even completed the official Northern Ireland Panini sticker album, buying and swapping stickers in secret with equally excited fans online, fully aware that men in their late-20's are not Panini's target audience. The Euros might not have needed me, but I needed them. A bit of rain wasn't going to stop me.

I flicked into autopilot. In a split second that pesky corner of my brain telling me to feel sorry for myself was shut down. I opened my tool kit, tweaked the brakes with my Allen key to give me the feeling that I was at least doing something constructive, wolfed down a couple of cereal bars and climbed back onto my rain-drenched saddle. It might be torture for the next twelve days, I said to myself as I began pedalling once again, but *nothing* was going to get between me and Nice.

2000 miles. Further than London to Moscow. When you think about it like that, it suddenly seems a fairly long way.

To make matters worse, I'm no Chris Froome or Geraint Thomas. My typical weekend cycle is fifteen miles to a café or chippy, stopping for an hour or so, and then fighting to turn the pedals under the weight of the glorious, greasy goodness I've just consumed.

I was actually eating cake half way through a cycle when the Euro 2016 draw was made in December 2015. That was when I was first struck with the idea. It's amazing the number of ideas for intense, physically-demanding challenges I come up with when I'm stuffing my face with junk food. Must be something to do with the effect of sugar or fat on the brain. I'd be willing to bet that Isaac Newton was munching on a slab of Victoria sponge when he was cracked on the head with that apple.

Out the teams came one at a time as I anxiously followed the draw on my phone. Germany, the world champions. Poland, with more goals scored in qualifying than any other nation thanks to Robert Lewandowski – arguably the most clinical striker on the planet at that time. And Ukraine, with their capital city that always makes me think of chicken.

We didn't expect it to be easy, though that was about as rough a line-up as we could possibly have landed. But while interesting, knowing our opponents didn't affect our fledgling holiday plans. The main concern for us fans was the list of venues. We all had fingers crossed for at least one trip to Paris. Because what's a trip to France without some selfies from the top of the Eiffel Tower? Information continued to trickle through at a painfully slow rate on my cutting-edge, seven-year old iPhone 3. It was fantastic news when it arrived though. First up were the Poles on the sun-drenched Cote d'Azur in Nice, followed four days later by a potentially winnable duel with Ukraine in Lyon, en route to taking on the might of Germany in Paris.

Immediately it just made sense to me. Here I was, shovelling chocolate cake into my mouth on a picnic bench outside a pub in the South of England. My bike was resting against a wall beside me. Why not do this in France? Why not re-enact this exact scenario every single day while charging along the roads between the three Northern Ireland games in the summer?

Six months later, and I was standing outside the gates of Windsor Park early on a grey, overcast Saturday morning towards the end of May. The leaving party of my mum, dad, brother-in-law and nephew were there, passing bits of breakfast between them as I played around with the height of the seatpost on my bike and the length of my helmet straps. It's strange (and more than a little bit sad), but it's a habit all cyclists seem to be born with. Unnecessarily fiddling with things that are absolutely fine as they are. Go to any cycling or triathlon event the world over and you'll see an obsessive army of 'fiddlers' an hour before they take off. I reckon I was just doing my best to delay the inevitable and pretend that I wasn't about to start a three-week cycling marathon.

We strode over to the fresh-faced security guard at the gates and asked if we could have a photo inside the stadium before leaving. "Can't see why that would be a problem, I'll just go and ask my boss," he chimed in his broad Belfast accent. Fantastic. Get this photo taken, send it to the papers, and we're up and running. Before long, a much taller, much older and much more imposing security guard appeared. For a moment I wondered if that's maybe how they determine hierarchy in the big, bad world of security guards. You're only allowed to be someone's boss if you're physically larger than them.

"Afraid we can't let you near the pitch, son."

The final Northern Ireland home match before the Euros, a morale-boosting win against Belarus, had been played on it the night before, with an on-pitch fireworks display and a lap of honour after full time. There were literally thousands of people in the stands only a few hours back. Surely I could twist his arm.

"Not even for a few seconds?"

"Nope. It's all being ripped up, you see."

I knew extensive stadium renovations had been ongoing for well over a year, but ripping up the pitch at 8am the morning after a match? Seemed far-fetched to me. I took the big lad's word for it anyway and smiled.

"I don't mind," I said. "It's just a quick photo I'm after. You know, to send out to the press. I'm cycling to France from here."

His face contorted into a peculiar shape, and he looked me up and down once again. It was clear he'd decided long ago that he wasn't in the mood to help me out.

"Nah, not today. Wouldn't look good in the papers with no grass there."

There was only so long I could postpone my departure. I ended up settling for a quick photo outside the locked gates of Windsor, looking like I was trapped in some sort of outdoor prison cell. Before I turned to leave, the (larger, angrier) security guard asked for my name and phone number. A small part of me naively assumed that, deep down, he was a compassionate soul, someone who would send encouraging messages of support as I pedalled along the French roads over the coming weeks. He didn't. I have a feeling those details got handed to the police immediately.

After he grunted and turned away to continue his crucial work of stopping people looking at the removal of turf, his smaller, friendlier accomplice whispered, "Here, if you're quick, I'll let you inside the gates before you go." What a hero, I thought. One of them's on my side at least. The photo was taken, the gate was removed from sight without any need for Photoshop, and I started pedalling to a small but heartening ripple of applause from my fan club, including the young security guard as its newest member.

I clicked through the gears as I rode through the tunnel of red, white and blue bunting flapping over Donegall Avenue, then followed the sharp bends onto the familiar surroundings of Tate's Avenue. It's the same beautiful red-brick stretch of road that I've walked with droves of fans in green and white before Northern Ireland matches for years. This morning it felt very different though. A chill swept through the air, and I pulled on my gloves at the first traffic lights I came to.

Setting off along Donegall Avenue, with over 2000 miles ahead of me

This was it. Six months of mentally plotting the route, and now I was on the road. I'd largely kept my plans to myself until this point. Part of me felt frightened of potential damage to any reputation I had as a cyclist if I didn't make it beyond the second day (and there was a fair chance of that considering I'd never done two long days of cycling back to back in my life, let alone twenty-one). There had also been the small matter of revising for medical school finals, which took place in mid-May and cramming for those had consumed most evenings for the couple of months prior to my departure. There hadn't been any intensive training programme, that's for sure.

Early that morning on the roads of South Belfast, there was no great fanfare. None of the small number and friends and family who knew about my trip were lining the street, and no-one coming out of the shops with their groceries knew who I was or what I was embarking on. But I liked that. Off on the adventure of a lifetime, and I was the only one who knew about it.

Just then the light turned green, and I pushed on down the road.

Crossing the border after a quick ham and cheese sandwich in Newry, at a coffee shop far too trendy for its surroundings, I felt surprisingly fresh. And I hate cheese. Can't stand the stuff. But as eating was something I'd have to do more and more of as the mile count ticked up, early training in how to stomach unpleasant, calorific foods seemed a smart move.

Once I got moving again, the roads were chaotic. Busier than a beehive being shaken by a hungry bear. Definitely not designed for bikes. The hard shoulders had puncture-loving stones and shards of glass scattered across them, but were the only safe place to cycle. Dodging those brutes turned a long, flat stretch of dual carriageway into an obstacle course. With all sorts of unfriendly vehicles blitzing past at a furious pace.

Occasionally I'd see inviting cycle path signs, allowing me to peel away from the white noise into an oasis of calm for a few miles. The only problem being that they took me off on tangents into the back end of nowhere. So I ended up faced with the dilemma of carrying on shuddering over a gauntlet of potholes towards my planned destination, or choosing the relative comfort of cycle paths that were more likely to take me to Middle Earth than Drogheda.

I imagined how much easier life would be if I was Dutch. They've got cycle paths coming out of their ears. Apparently there are more bicycles in the Netherlands than there are people, and one in three Dutch people cycle as their main mode of transport (compared to only 2% of people in the UK and Ireland). I tried to forget about how much of a pummelling my wrists were taking holding my bike straight on this rugged hard shoulder, and dreamed I was sailing along a riverbank in Amsterdam. It wasn't long before I snapped out of my daydream with an arrogant smirk on my face when I remembered that Holland's football team – packed with household names like Sneijder, Robben and van Persie – had fallen short in their attempt to qualify for the Euros. You might well have your windmills and blonde-haired supermodels and clogs and speed skaters and purpose-built cycle paths, but at least we know how to play footy.

The heat was intensifying. I'd already stopped twice to slap on sunscreen by the time I passed through Dundalk's bustling streets. Irish tricolours waved in the breeze from almost every building. The sort of size of flags you could use if you were ever running low on tablecloths at a family gathering. The constituency office of Gerry Adams, bushy-bearded republican politician and not exactly the biggest lover of all things Northern Ireland, came into view on my left as I freewheeled along West Street. Everywhere I looked pubs were advertising Euro 2016, displaying colours of every competing nation except for one notable exception.

"How long do you reckon I'd have survived back there in my NI shirt?" I asked Dad as we stopped at the next village for a pit stop.

Mum and Dad had followed me down from Belfast. Clearly the temptation of driving at 15mph for three days to the south coast of Ireland was too great for them, and so I had the luxury of a support car over that stretch. Not exactly Team Sky, but to be fair I don't think Team Sky would be supplying their cyclists with iced buns and triple chocolate muffins every twenty miles.

"They probably wouldn't have been inviting you in for a drink," said Dad.

"Did you see if Gerry was out cheering me on?"

"Not today. Suppose it is the weekend after all."

After making use of the toilet at the local vet's, I shuffled awkwardly past a very unhappy German Shepherd in the waiting room and climbed back onto my wheels of steel. From there I pumped my tiring thighs a little longer past the striking beauty of Castlebellingham and up the steady climb through Dunleer, before rolling to the finish line of day one on the footbridge over the River Boyne in Drogheda.

Day One in the bag, propping myself up over the Boyne

The three of us congregated in the car-park of a picturesque riverside restaurant, owned by a certain Mr McDonald, and celebrated with a round of McFlurrys. Eighty-five miles under the belt. My legs felt tight. It's only when you get off the bike and stop pedalling for ten minutes that it properly hits you.

I grimaced as I did a couple of those hold-your-ankle-behind-your-bum manoeuvres that are supposed to help your quads. To be honest, this was really just me showing off for the Drogheda locals, considering my post-exercise stretches usually consist of bending down to untie my laces, reaching forward to open the fridge and lunging in the direction of the sofa.

Really what I needed (and wanted) most was a bed. What we got – once we arrived at our B&B – was a garage. One of those cramped buildings where lawnmowers, toolboxes and half-empty paint cans go to gather dust. Not just for my bike, but for us to sleep in. Three single beds had been packed in, and a few brightly-coloured paintings stuck on the walls to cover over the cracks. Irish entrepreneurship at its finest.

Thankfully, it was only half past three in the afternoon so there was plenty of time to lie in a vegetative state eating curry for the rest of the day. And then sleep. Like a baby that had been fed a cocktail of sleeping pills. When I finally woke up eleven hours later on Sunday morning, there was a thick sheet of condensation over my quilt, as tends to happen when sleeping in a garage. A few painful, half-hearted stretches and a fried breakfast later, I staggered in the direction of my saddle of pain once more. Sunday mass was in full swing, so the roads were dead and I raced down to Dublin far quicker than anticipated. The temperature had cranked up another notch from the day before, and the sun grilled my already burnt skin.

I found myself repeatedly cycling past wonderfully stereotypical Irish farmers (complete with flat caps and heavy, tweed blazers despite the baking heat) on country roads. Having sailed past four or five standing at various bus shelters that morning. I soon learnt to start chatting about fifty metres before I reached them, to complete the lengthy conversations they all insisted on having.

Approaching one such local at a dilapidated bus stop in Balbriggan, I sat up and bellowed "Morning, how's it going?"

"Aye, not too bad at all now. What about yourself?" came the hearty response.

"Great thanks."

"Lovely weather now isn't it?" he continued.

"Definitely is," I'd say, my farmer friend now well behind me.

"Where are you heading today then?" came an increasingly distant voice, seemingly oblivious to the fact he was now fast becoming a dot on the horizon as I craned my neck to look at him.

"Off to France," I shouted, interested to hear what he thought of my optimistic travel plans. He struck me as the sort of gent who'd never been beyond the boundaries of his village before. I wouldn't be in any way surprised if you told me that he never actually got on the bus, and instead just passed his time standing at the bus shelter every day talking to strangers about nothing in particular. I could just about make out his reply as his lilting voice danced in the wind behind me.

"Good lad, you might as well, sure it's the perfect day for it."

Our wee country.

Three words that fill me with joy.

It's mad really. For the vast majority of time that I've been a fan of the Northern Ireland football team, we've been extremely average. Bang average. Most of our fans would admit that, while continuing to belt out ironic anthems about how similar we are to Brazil. But, at heart, something remains in all of us that believes we *can* be world-beaters. We're deluded by hope.

And it was this hope sustaining me in early 2016 prior to university finals. Through long hours and late nights in the library, my only respite from learning about causes of bleeding from the back passage or the anatomy of the blood supply to the brain was opening a world atlas from time to time and plotting how I could cycle to cheer twenty-three warriors to glory in France.

People in my generation (I'm thirty years old) have been raised on misty-eyed stories about Gerry Armstrong's volley against Spain in 1982, Norman Whiteside becoming the youngest player to feature at a World Cup, Pat Jennings' shovel-sized hands, that time George Best nutmegged Johan Cruyff, and how Northern Ireland remain British champions from the last tournament of its kind in 1984. I've lost count of the number of times my granny has told me how she knocked her mum off the armchair celebrating a Northern Ireland goal at the 1958 World Cup as they gathered around the family radio.

We want new nostalgic stories to pass on. Many of us had accepted that we'd probably witnessed our generation's 'moment' in 2005 when David Healy (who I still have a signed poster of on my bedroom wall – along with a signed pair of boots and a signed football top – to be fair, there's not much I own that doesn't have his name scrawled across it) sunk the English, in arguably the most memorable sporting event of my life. But even that was only a qualifying match which, again, sadly amounted to nothing.

I even had a rabbit called Healy. The obsession was real.

Dramatic highpoints have been few and far between though. Too often in recent years following Northern Ireland has involved watching through cracks in our fingers while awe-inspiring wins are backed up by yet more inevitable defeats against world superpowers like Albania, Azerbaijan and Luxembourg.

Sitting with the map of France spread in front of me and a cup of tea in my hand, I began planning my potential trip. You might think that a venture so substantial would involve weeks of meticulous organising and deliberating between different options for equipment and accommodation. You'd be wrong. I had a route scribbled down within an hour, on the back of some old notes about the risk factors for Type 2 diabetes.

Adopting a novel approach to route planning, I held my thumb and index finger apart to represent one hundred miles on the map, and moved steadily from Belfast all the way to Nice, jotting down whichever city, town or village my thumb/finger landed nearest to on the atlas. Two weeks was the time-frame I settled on to make my way to the Cote d'Azur en vélo and join the tribe in time for kick off.

Going to Windsor Park in Belfast to take in an international match with the Green and White Army (or GAWA, as our fanbase is affectionately known) is a unique and addictive pastime. Take a glimpse first hand and you'll never be the same again. I know many converts who claimed they hated everything about football, before one wintery evening of standing buried beneath an overpriced scarf from the merchandise stall and singing along to Neil Diamond with emotionally-liberated, middle-aged men changed the course of their lives forever.

I lived in England for seven years as a student, and I always felt sorry for English football fans. Their national sport just didn't seem to make them happy. It occasionally encouraged a disreputable minority to lob beer bottles and chairs in city squares on their travels, but it didn't ever appear to leave the main bulk of them with a sense of contentment or pride. At least not until Gareth Southgate reintroduced some optimism with his squad's unexpected march to the 2018 World Cup semi-finals.

Their issue is that they constantly look back to that sun-tinged World Cup win in 1966, lifting the Jules Rimet trophy under Wembley's twin towers, and assume they've still got Bobby Charlton and Geoff Hurst playing for them. They don't. They've got Jordan Henderson and Jamie Vardy. And until they win big tournaments again, *if* that ever happens, they seem destined to remain trapped in a never-ending cycle of grief about enduring thirty/forty/fifty etc. years of hurt.

Just seeing our team in action creates a buzz like no other in our quirky little corner of this island. What might once have been seen (rightly or wrongly) as a team for only Protestant quarters of the population to get behind is now very much an all-inclusive team at the forefront of a new, modern chapter in Northern Ireland's sporting history, alongside other widely-supported icons like Rory McIlroy and Carl Frampton.

Songs bursting with trademark, self-deprecatory humour echo around the stands. Ninety-five percent of our chants are about ourselves, with the remainder (unsuccessful) attempts to unsettle our opposition. A few years ago Cristiano Ronaldo came to Belfast with Portugal, and was taunted mercilessly all night with cries of

"You're just a cheap Gareth Bale" and "Messi, Messi, Messi!" Needless to say, he scored a hat-trick and single-handedly decimated our defence. Running to the North Stand filled with home fans, he celebrated by throwing his head back, arms held aloft. Stunned into silence, the stadium soon rose to its feet to give the cheeky scamp the ovation he deserved.

German World Cup winner and honorary member of the GAWA, Mats Hummels, even admitted prior to Euro 2016 that his native fans have "a little stretch to go before being on a par with the Northern Ireland fans." The most trouble you'll stumble upon at a game in Belfast today is going hoarse from singing 'We're not Brazil, we're Northern Ireland' for the sixteenth time, or needing a few puffs on your inhaler after doing the 'bouncy' more than your embarrassingly low fitness levels will allow.

Without doubt the best fans in the world.

Dublin caught me by surprise. Extremely easy to get into on a bike, and extremely hard to get out of. I cruised into the heart of the city before I properly noticed where I was. Sailing down O'Connell Street in the most glorious sunshine I think I've ever seen north or south of the border, the General Post Office came into view in its imposing Georgian pomp. Impressive it may well be, but a tad excessive for a post office. I mean, the one I send my letters from in Coleraine sits hidden behind a dingy window in the back of a Spar in the same aisle as the custard creams and reduced loaves of bread.

My skin tingled in the baking heat from the early-afternoon sun. This was not the Ireland I'd seen in postcard pictures of Dublin. I dismounted on one of the city-centre bridges over the Liffey and applied another generous layer of Factor 50 to my increasingly pink forearms. Tourists shuffled past wearing summer dresses and sunglasses. If this is what Ireland is like, I thought to myself, just wait until I hit France. I'm going to end up with a farmer's tan to last a lifetime.

The GPO, Dublin

The roads wriggling around the heart of the city were the cycling equivalent of Chinese water torture in their agonising complexity. The first time I cycled past St Stephen's Green I stopped to take a selfie, over the moon to have discovered a picturesque park with my name on it. The fourth time I cycled past St Stephen's Green, I'd decided that I never wanted to see it again for as long as I live.

After escaping the capital's clutches (thanks largely to the help of another cyclist trying to do the same thing), I scampered along the open road past the University College campus heading south. A wave of relief swept over me as it dawned on me that I wouldn't see another big city until I crossed the Channel. Urban life is fun, don't get me wrong. As long as a bicycle isn't involved. On two wheels, cities morph into angry beasts. Every corner you take, a new set of six lanes appears for you to choose from. Pick the wrong option, and you'll get chewed up by impatient traffic in an instant.

At Bray, I took the opportunity to swing left in the direction of the coast for the remainder of the ride down to Arklow. Gorgeous rays of late-afternoon sunshine bounced off the Irish Sea as I sped along quiet, weaving roads high above Brittas Bay. When scenery and weather combine like this, you feel sorry for people who don't cycle. It's a world apart. Prescriptions for it should genuinely be dished out on the NHS. Nothing clears your head like it.

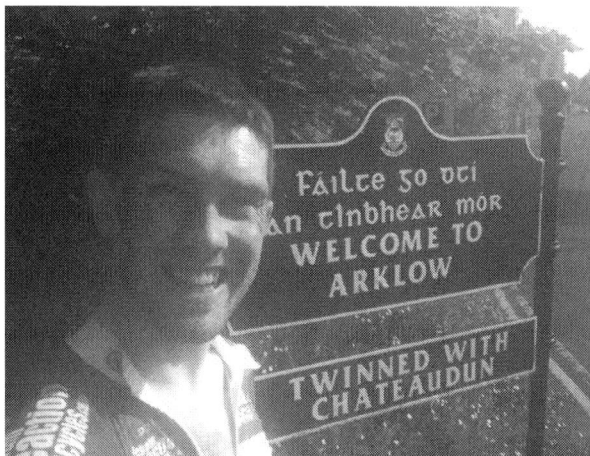

Arriving in Arklow for my last stopover before the ferry

Drinking my second mug of hot chocolate in our cottage in Arklow that evening, Mum emerged from the hallway displaying a selection of new clothes that she'd raided from a bike shop earlier in the day.

"OK, so I've got you some gloves."

"Got a pair already, Mum."

"Well these ones are yellow. You might as well bring both."

"I've a limited amount of space, you do realise?" I said, scribbling another answer into the crossword in Dad's newspaper as she continued.

"What about a coat? I've bought you a coat as well."

"Have you seen the weather the past few days? I don't need a coat. It's only gonna get warmer the further down France I go."

"Stephen, you *need* a coat. I'm putting it in your bag."

With the benefit of hindsight, Mum's stubbornness may have saved my life on this occasion. I'd soon discover that the weather in France was going to hit me like a water cannon to the face. I remember chatting to a friend in England a couple of years ago about how often we turned to our mums for advice, and his jaw hit the floor when I said I phoned mine every night. Sometimes for half a minute, sometimes for half an hour. Ask almost any Northern Irish person fortunate enough to still have a mother, and they'll give you a similar answer. We'd be sunk without them.

The following morning I had a ferry to catch, so time was of the essence. I threw my panniers into my parents' car, flicked into racing mode and time-trialled the forty miles over undulating country roads into Wexford. The heat was less intense than the previous two days, and I could taste the adrenaline with the freedom of the smooth, rural lanes ahead of me.

Within a couple of hours I rolled up to the sandy beach at Rosslare, and dipped my feet in the water. Belfast to the South Coast in just over two days. Suddenly France didn't seem quite so massive. I loaded my bike onto the ferry, and made my way to the back balcony of the ship. One long blast of the ship's horn, and we edged away from the harbour. I could just about make out Mum and Dad running across the rocks waving hankies, like the end credits from an old black and white movie.

When they disappeared from view, I grabbed a chicken burger from the restaurant and slinked back to my cheap, windowless cabin on the fourth floor. I knew that the next time I set foot on dry land, it would be just me. No support crew. Nobody speaking my language. Just me, cycling on the other side of the road, on a mission to follow my boyhood heroes around France.

My relationship with technology is a complicated one. It's not like I'm avoiding it. I really want things to work between us, but I guess it's not meant to be. One of my cycling buddies from university had heard an early draft of plans for my trip and had lent me his satnav. It'll be just like hopping on an exercise bike, I said at the time. It's impossible to get lost with a satnav.

Now allow me to invite you a step further into my world. Methodical preparation and forward thinking are not aspects of my character that will feature highly when my obituary is written one day. I didn't take the satnav out of its box until I got off the ship in France. And suddenly, there I was. Freezing my chops off while struggling to balance the bike between my legs due to the sheer weight of the pannier bags on either side.

The satnav switched on, which was nice. But I didn't have the first idea what to do with it from that point on. I spotted a van with English writing on it, and made a beeline for it. Unfortunately the people in it were Australian. They listened momentarily to my plea for help with half-baked expressions on their faces, before abandoning my concerns and rambling on about their holiday plans instead. All the while calling me maaaaeeeeettttt at the end of every sentence. Look, if all you're gonna do is chat about surfing and the sick new paintwork on the side of your van, I don't know if we're realistically going to be maaaaeeeeettttts. And no I haven't met your sister Donna who moved to Dublin earlier this year. We're not all related. Why, do you know Rolf Harris?

I shuffled away and propped my bike against a nearby fence, with Guns N' Roses blaring from the Aussie campervan behind me. Flicking the little plastic buttons pathetically, it became clear that the satnav was only going to show a maximum of two miles at a time on its puny screen, and that wasn't exactly going to cut the mustard when I needed to churn out in the region of a hundred miles each day.

I disposed the satnav deep into the darkest recess of my front pannier bag (inside the tube of my emergency toilet roll) and unbuckled one of the rear panniers. Moments before leaving the south coast of Ireland, Dad had insisted I take an atlas with me. A huge, bulky A3 book that I clearly didn't have room for. Each page went into remarkable detail, from the smallest villages in France to the most sprawling, vibrant cities. This atlas was an old relic hanging around from family camping trips in my teenage years, and so out of politeness – and not much else – I took it from Dad and shoved it in amongst my other possessions.

Having found the well-thumbed page with Cherbourg on it, I carefully ripped it from the atlas, folded it in three, and slipped it under the plastic rain-cover on top of my front pannier. Best to get moving in vaguely the right direction, I thought to myself. I quickly realised, though, that cycle paths weren't going to carry me there. All the roads leaving Cherbourg looked fairly heavy-duty. A motorway seemed to be my only option for the first ten miles. Surely that couldn't be the case. I decided that since I've come this far, I might as well try my hand. Worst case scenario, the French peelers will come after me. I pulled on my fluorescent yellow coat, put on my back light and veered off at the junction for the main road leaving Cherbourg.

As I fought to spin the pedals along the uphill stretch before me, heavy drops of rain started falling from overhead. Before long it was drumming down. I mean a rainshower of biblical proportions. The weight of the panniers and the tight incline took me by surprise, and I quickly developed that horrible burning sensation in the back of the throat that you normally only get after vigorous exercise. Not exactly what you want five minutes into cycling the length of France. This is purgatory, I mumbled to myself, as I used my left palm as a windscreen wiper to remove some of the driving rain from my face.

After ten miles of living on a tightrope between slipping into a ditch on one side and being flattened by a speeding lorry on the other, I peeled off into the first small town I could find – called Valognes – where I came crashing back down to earth with a bump.

The wound in my leg stung with every new drop of rain that hit it. Having only ever had two very minor bike accidents in my life prior to this trip, I wasn't anticipating a crash inside my first hour on foreign soil. Mind you, a small part of me kind of liked parading such an impressive battle scar to the watching world. Bonjour mes copains, take a look at me and give me the respect that I am due. You might think I'm a hopelessly lost tourist who should have noticed that slightly raised, slippery metal kerb at the side of the road before mounting it, but you'd be wrong. I am a modern-day adventurer, ready to bleed for my country. You know the people in that Tour de France race you all love to watch? Well I'm basically one of them, only I use Fanta and flapjacks instead of EPO.

Normandy remains intertwined with military history – synonymous with unmentionable suffering around the D-day landings into Nazi-occupied Northern France in 1944. I took a slight detour from my planned route to experience the sobering sight of endless rows of small, cross-shaped headstones at the German War Cemetery in Orglandes. The resting place for the bodies of over ten thousand young German men, almost all much younger than me when they met their untimely death. So many of them misinformed and misguided. I couldn't help but reflect on the tragedy of these lives packed with potential being sacrificed because of the greed and manipulation of those in power over them. It might occasionally be necessary in exceptional circumstances, but there's no denying that war is an awful, awful thing.

I consulted my map and made tracks in the direction of Bayeux. The rain was giving me a pummelling now. There was no place to hide. Every road I ventured onto appeared to cut through wide-open plains of exposed grassland, with no shelter from trees or buildings whatsoever.

Every time I pulled in to check directions I noticed my teeth chattering from the bitter chill in the air. Stopping for decent breaks was no longer an option. Having pushed on for as long as I physically could in the ever-worsening downpour, I dumped my bike against the window of a village bakery, grabbed my wallet from the front pannier and ran inside.

The middle-aged husband and wife who ran the shop couldn't speak a button of English, so I repeatedly jabbed my rain-soaked finger against the glass on their counter and asked "Qu'est que c'est?" for each and every item on sale. I eventually heard the word *poire* and stopped them in their tracks, holding up three grubby fingers and saying "Trois, s'il vous plait". I scoffed down the first of my pear-filled pastries while explaining that I was aiming for Bayeux. They tried to talk me out of it for my own safety – feeling the remaining 40km was too far at this time of the evening (with it now past seven o'clock) and in this weather – but I made it clear that I couldn't afford to slacken off, knowing full well that this was only the very first step on my road to Nice.

This delightful, bickering married couple then scribbled village by village directions to Bayeux on a paper bag while sneakily throwing another free pastry into a box for the road. Their insistence on going out of their way to lend a hand made me think they could have just as easily been from Northern Ireland as Northern France.

Back in the saddle, the roads were now coated in a sheet of water at least a few centimetres deep. Spray from the tarmac lashed over my back with every revolution of my wheels, and I could hardly see with the persistent rainwater driving headlong into my face. After what seemed like a lifetime of debating whether I'd rather curl up in a ball and expire peacefully by the side of road or continue with this punishment, a sign welcoming me to Bayeux came into view.

Creaking open the gate and squelching along the garden path, I knocked the door where I was met by Eliane and her husband, Jean-Yves. With the rain having broken the phone in my back pocket (where their address was saved), it's a miracle I found their place at all. Warmth from the fire in their living room hit me like a cushion as the door creaked open. They very quickly analysed my pitiful state, and shepherded me towards their garage door to avoid bringing some of The Great Flood Part II into their pristine semi-detached abode.

In a not entirely non-threatening way, they requested that I remove all items of wet clothing before setting foot in their house. Which just so happened to be everything I had on. I stripped down to my bib shorts, hung the rest of my saturated clothes on a washing line in their garage, and trundled to my bedroom wearing a pair of fluffy pink slippers they'd thrust into my hands.

Before we go any further, I just want to say it wasn't my fault that they'd furnished the bedroom floor with a gleaming white carpet. If you're into cycling, here's a little word of warning: chain oil is a great way to lose friends quickly. It sneaks on to your fingers, clothes and equipment unannounced, and before you know it you've plastered a permanent smear across your great-granny's family heirloom of a curtain that was once valued for £10,000 on Antiques Roadshow. Chain oil is a colossal pain in the rear. And there's no delete option once it has made its mark.

Which explains my heart plummeting into my shoes when Eliane's beaming smile turned rapidly to a shriek as she pointed at the carpet yelling 'Noir, noir!' followed by some high-pitched squeals only audible to four-legged domestic animals. My French interpretation's not the best, but as she yelped furiously down the stairs to her husband, I could tell she was raining down curses upon me. She scurried away and returned half a minute later with a tub of bicarbonate of soda.

She pushed the small, red tub into my shivering hands, and looked at me. I looked back at her. I didn't even know what bicarbonate of soda was. Maybe she wanted me to bake something for her by way of apology. She pointed her index finger at the black smear on the floor (caused by one of my pannier bags it turns out), and so I sprinkled some of the contents on to the carpet. I grabbed a cloth from my bag, and rubbed as hard as my exhausted arms would allow. I could hear her breathing over me like Darth Vader with a chest infection.

"Aaaah, c'est très bien, non?" I said a couple of minutes later, standing up with a hopeful expression on my face.

It didn't *really* look very good. To be honest, it looked exactly the same. Eliane wasn't convinced, and after pointedly telling me where the shower was and throwing me a towel, she stomped back down the stairs. The fact that my hosts now hated me only concerned me for about five minutes, because it was then that I reached the bathroom. As soon as the water started running, I slumped to the floor of the shower. Sitting in a ball of grime and fatigue, I can't tell you how magical life was for the following half an hour. My thighs burned, the skin between my legs was as raw as freshly-bought sandpaper and I was emotionally spent from navigating my way around chaotic traffic on unfamiliar roads all day, but at least it was over for now.

After cleaning myself up, all I wanted to do was sleep. But I knew I had to eat to have something in the tank for the next day. So I ventured out in the torrential rain once more, and found a posh, candlelit restaurant across the street from the Bayeux tapestry.

There I sat, surrounded by three couples on dates who clearly felt more than a little bit awkward at the sight of the pasty, sunburnt foreigner sat on his own with no friends and no clothes other than mud-speckled trackie bottoms and a mesh cycling jersey. Eating a pizza with an egg on top.

Living the dream.

One problem with cycling blindly through a foreign country with only a scrap of paper pointing you from village to village is that you have no concrete idea of how long a journey will take. Each square on my map represented ten kilometres, and once I factored in getting lost several times passing through every village and never quite managing to travel in a straight line, I learnt that I could roughly cover two squares per hour. For example, Bayeux to Rouen clocked in at around 180km (or eighteen squares), which meant I set off that morning knowing I had in the region of nine hours of cycling to factor in.

Unfortunately it wasn't always that simple.

You set out thinking that travelling at an average of 20km/hr (or 12-ish mph) will be a piece of cake, then out of nowhere you get bludgeoned by four hours of unwavering headwinds, or you get a puncture (or two), or you have to go a handful of miles off course to find a supermarket to top up food and drinks supplies. Media interest had also emerged from home, and I was suddenly in demand. BBC Radio Ulster were keen to chat every couple of days on their breakfast current affairs show, and my local radio station had asked for daily interviews just before lunchtime. I loved these excuses for a revitalising dose of Norn Irish banter – and exposure for my chosen charity – but it did mean factoring in even more time out of the saddle.

I could only carry two bottles at any one time, and these forever needed topping up. Which meant shops of all shapes and sizes became very sought-after commodities. Having discovered a hypermarché on the outskirts of Caen, I locked my bike and marched inside with pannier bags draped over my shoulder.

I'm not a fussy shopper. One 1.5 litre bottle of Fanta Exotic and I was at the till with cash in hand. Just then, our friend behind the counter spoke a string of words that no-one from the right side of the English Channel would have had a chance of understanding. I was flattered that she thought I was already carrying off the 'French look' to a sufficient degree that she even expected me to have a clue.

I smiled innocently and mumbled "Mon francais, c'est pas bien. J'ai un vélo. Je suis fatigué. Je voudrais le Fanta." Turns out she thought I'd nicked half the goods from her shelves in my pannier bags. It'd be interesting to know how many shoplifters she's had recently wearing fluorescent yellow jackets and skintight lycra shorts. Thanks to the shop manager being swiftly drafted in as a translator, a full and comprehensive search was conducted of my person and my belongings in front of a long and increasingly impatient queue, in which they found nothing more exciting than my bog roll, four unopened packs of ibuprofen, and the two rusty teaspoons I've used for years as my makeshift puncture repair kit.

Later that afternoon, passing over the rolling hills beyond Epaignes, the spoons were thrust into action for the first time with a back wheel blowout. Thick mist descended as I prised the tyre off down a country lane. By the time I was back in business, it was early evening and I was still thirty miles short of Rouen. There wasn't a hope I'd make it to Rouen for 10pm, let alone my intended time of 7pm. I texted my host to apologise, especially since she'd promised a three-course meal. She'd even invited an old friend of hers around for dinner with us. I felt a slight pang of guilt, but my circumstances couldn't be changed. All I could do was focus on keeping the head down and driving my pedals one rotation at a time.

Roads are scary places for cyclists at the best of times. But when you're lost in a strange country, you're hungry and your legs are simultaneously burning from fatigue and shivering from the cold (and it's starting to turn dark), roads are urgent-need-for-new-underwear-level terrifying. Lorries and motorbikes and cars endlessly career past, their horn blasts providing a soundtrack to the obscenities yelled by their drivers. And all the while, I'm there hugging the right-hand side of the road for all I'm worth. My eyes almost burn a hole in the tarmac as I focus intensely on maintaining no more than a three inch gap between my front wheel and the white line.

The end of the long road to Rouen, outside the city's train station

By the time I arrived on the outskirts of Rouen, light was slipping fast from the gloomy June sky. When I finally meandered into the city centre and located Sylvie's house it was as black as a panther who'd done ten lengths in a swimming pool full of oil. I shuffled towards the red wooden door, took the phone out of my front pannier and called my host for the evening one last time.

I glanced up at the cracks in the doorframe as the phone rang, a sharp wind catching me off guard while I stood in the cobbled alleyway outside her house. Nobody answered the phone, but I could make out footsteps. All of a sudden, the door was thrown open, and Sylvie's beaming smile lit up the night sky.

"Stephen! So good to finally meet you, come in! You look so cold."

"Thank you. Merci. Merci beaucoup." Even in the semi-frozen state I was in, it was encouraging to hear my fluent French hadn't deserted me. "Where can I leave the bike?"

"Just bring it through. It'll be safe round the back"

Sylvie took a handful of steps, and I followed through the doorway into a pristine back garden, roughly the size of a snooker table and about as well manicured. A cat darted across the grass and through a catflap in the kitchen door.

"That's so kind. Thank you"

"Come in, Stephen. Please."

I stepped inside, unsuccessfully balancing with one hand on the radiator while I clumsily took off my sodden shoes and socks.

"Where have you journeyed from?"

"Bayeux."

"Ou?"

"From Bayeux. Avec le tapestry". Here's a tip. If ever in doubt on the continent, just put 'le' before the word you don't know, and say it with a touch of false confidence and a flamboyant French accent. Works a treat.

"No, no, I know Bayeux, but that's so far...how many days have you taken?"

"Just today. Left early this morning."

"Ca n'est pas possible."

"That's exactly what the woman in the last place said!" I blurted, unashamedly proud that I'd succeeded in making the impossible possible, if only for one day.

To be fair, her words were exactly what I would have said a few months earlier too. But as the days went on, I was realising more and more what could be achieved by breaking huge challenges into manageable chunks. Impossible can very quickly become possible by turning one big thing into ten smaller things. Over the past four or five years I've taken part in endurance events (marathons and long-distance triathlons), and what I have taken from them is exactly what I was being reminding of on the roads of France. Break the task down and set small targets. Keep going to the next corner, or the next village, or the next snack break – but don't think further than that. Do whatever it takes (slow down, walk, crawl, stop for a rest), just don't give up.

Each evening, scrolling through dozens of Airbnb pictures taken from misleading angles, I would book the place to stay for the following night. It was an unpredictable but exciting way to travel, for you have no real idea who or what who you're going to be faced with on arrival. But after my first properly long day in the saddle, Sylvie was the perfect host. She pointed me in the direction of the bathroom, and told me to return to the kitchen for dinner in five minutes.

As I creaked the kitchen door open after washing several layers of urban filth from my skin, the most amazing cocktail of smells hit me all at once. Sylvie was standing by the cooker, stirring a pot of pea soup and sprinkling in some salt and herbs for good measure. She said the soup might need a couple more minutes, and offered me a beer.

I obliged. It would have been rude not to. What she didn't explain was that it was an over-sized bottle of 8% strength local craft beer, so I tried to take slow sips and discreetly scoff as much bread as I could to dampen the alcohol's effects on my empty stomach after one hundred and fifteen miles on the road.

Soon I was presented with enough soup to feed a family. Instead of doling it out into bowls for us to share, Sylvie placed the entire pot of piping hot soup on a chopping board in front of me with one massive ladle. It was like a scene from Oliver. This was followed by a pot of spaghetti bolognese, and a dessert of achingly soft chocolate cake topped with rhubarb and strawberries. I did not deserve this. I hadn't paid for any of this. This lady was simply being a legend. If she wasn't a married woman and about thirty years older than me, I'd have kissed her there and then.

We spent the next two hours talking in half-French/half-English about everything from her children's university courses to the current political climate in Northern Ireland (which, to be fair, is hard enough to do in English). While I finished dessert, Sylvie nipped next door to find directions on her computer to help me on my way in the morning. I heard a clatter of plates behind me in the empty kitchen, and turned around in my seat.

"Ehh Sylvie…c'est un chat dans le…sink."

I didn't think I was seeing things. The beer wasn't *that* strong.

"Ah, c'est Tiguen" came the response from the other room, "He's my little companion. I think he likes you."

"He's having a bath in your sink," I replied. "Is that…normal?"

"Yes"

"Ok. He's now tucking into the cheese on your worktop. Is that normal?"

"Yes"

Fair enough. French people and their idiosyncrasies. Eating snails and frog legs, wearing onions as jewellery, and owning cheese-eating, amphibious cats as pets – just another standard day on the continent.

I chucked my last corner of chocolate cake in the vague direction of Tiguen as I walked out of the kitchen, and heard frantic splashing noises from the sink as I climbed the narrow, spiral staircase up to my room.

The Friday night after Easter, I'd been enjoying a beverage with two mates in our local pub back home. Spence and Jason are my main cycling companions (or as I like to call them, my domestiques) and that night felt like the right time in my tentative planning to throw out my idea of cycling to every NI game in France on two wheels.

"Haha whaaaaaaat?! Not a chance!" shrieked Jason in that eternally optimistic manner of his. With his PhD in Sports Science, he loves nothing more than dissecting the training programmes of athletic types around him, and wasn't entirely convinced that my weekly thirty-mile spin topped off with a fried breakfast was optimal preparation.

"A month is loads of time," I continued. "100 miles a day for a few weeks, that's do-able, right?"

"You'd need to have *at least* a six month training plan in place, with a couple of long cycles every week."

"I'm not trying to win the Tour de France here. It'll just be a gentle spin. No hassle."

I've known Jason since we attended cross country club as twelve year olds at school. Even back then, he was doing weird and wonderful hamstring stretches that the coaches hadn't even seen before. While he was consistently winning local races over middle and long distance, I could be found half way round the swamp-like courses stopping for a chat with the slower competitors and grabbing a bite to eat.

For better or for worse, not much has changed since then.

Spence, however, was intrigued by the idea. "Sounds decent. I wouldn't be able to get a month off work, but I could probably sort out a week".

I hadn't actually thought of bringing anyone. Not because I'm a hermit who likes sitting alone in dark rooms listening to Damien Rice songs, but I just didn't honestly believe anyone else would be interested in such a mad escapade.

Especially Spence, who *hates* football. Loves his cycling, but couldn't care much less about the beautiful game if he tried. But now he'd mentioned it, it began to dawn on me that a bit of company might not be the worst thing in the world.

"Where do you reckon you could fly to?" I asked Spence.

"Any big cities really. You going anywhere near Paris?"

Paris was the finish line, with our concluding group match there on the 21st June. That wouldn't be any use to Spence if he wanted to get some miles under his belt. I didn't have an itinerary set in stone at this point though, so it didn't seem the biggest chore to re-route slightly.

"I'm sure I could pick you up somewhere as I head south."

Jason (aka Doubting Thomas) leaned back in his chair, an amused smirk on his face, busy trying to calculate the average miles per hour I'd need to maintain along with the daily carbohydrate and protein requirements. All the while repeatedly shaking his head and mumbling "Not possible, Steve. Not possible".

This was a catalyst for me from that point on. Jason was the first person to say that this idea was impossible (although not the last). But in hindsight, I've got a lot to thank him for. I don't know if it was reverse psychology all along, but his certainty that I'd eventually pack it in gave me the impetus to push through the pain barrier over and over again when things were working against me on the road.

"No hard feelings, Steve, but you'll capitulate within the first week," he said throwing on his coat and grabbing his car keys from the table.

We drank up, played a couple of games of Pints Make Prizes on the quiz machine, and made our way home.

One recurring problem with cycling through French towns is the climb out of them. Maybe the founding fathers foresaw the invention of the bicycle and thought it would be a laugh to trap travellers by building their new settlements at the bottom of brutal hills. Or (more likely, let's be honest) it has something to do with proximity to water for trade routes. Either way it makes arriving into towns and cities unbridled joy, and leaving them pure torture.

Rouen is one of the biggest culprits of this phenomenon. Sylvie's house was perched on a hill high above the city centre, and I had thought that having that as a starting point might have saved my legs some extra altitude. To my dismay, my route away from Rouen was across the River Seine and out the other side, so it was a swift and heartbreaking descent to sea level before the struggle began once again for my poor, undeserving quads.

My French was still below par – to say I was becoming more fluent would be like saying Liam Neeson is becoming more convincing with American accents – but I was now managing to string together three or four sentences each time I met a native. Granted, they were the exact same three or four sentences, though it did allow me to say slightly more than "Bonjour". Eliane and Sylvie from the first couple of nights had graciously explained simple phrases to me so I could talk about my cycling trip in French, and from that point on meeting strangers would involve me clearing my throat, puffing out my chest ever so slightly and saying the following with casual bravado:

"Je suis dans un tour de France. Je fais du vélo de Belfast à Nice à Paris. J'adore le foot, et je vais regarder tous les matches de l'Irlande du Nord. Allez l'armée verte et blanche!"

For the uninitiated (much like I was before arriving on French soil): I'm on a tour around France, cycling from Belfast to Nice to Paris. I love football, and I'm heading to all the NI matches. Green and White Army!

The first lucky recipient of this monologue in Rouen was a binman cleaning the streets outside the cathedral. Amazing building by the way. I won't even pretend to know about architecture, but I can tell when a building takes my breath away. From the jagged Gothic design and intricate stone sculptures of its front façade to the central spire that's so ridiculously tall it looks like someone got mixed up with the measurements, it is a monumental sight to behold.

"Have you heard of Claude Monet?" asked the binman, before explaining how the prolific impressionist had once famously done a series of paintings of the cathedral.

I responded by asking him "Have you heard of Kyle Lafferty?" When he looked back blankly and shook his head, I explained that he was also a great artist. His confusion intensified. Needless to say, I left soon after.

Having negotiated the gruelling, almost-vertical escape route from the city, I sought shelter from the ceaseless winds in the form of the forest of Lyons. Long, long way from Lyon, so don't get the two confused if you're booking any French holidays soon. I faced the dilemma of wanting to wear more layers to stay warm, while simultaneously wanting to shed layers to reduce the amount of fabric flapping in the blizzard lashing against me. On reaching

Beauvais (complete with its own jaw-dropping church), I raided the first bakery I could find, leaving fifteen minutes later and two stone heavier.

My view from the saddle, each and every day

A mesh of tricky junctions appeared as I attempted to follow the road out of Beauvais, and I stopped to consider my options. Just then, two elderly ladies shuffled out of a clothes shop close to the traffic lights. I decided this was my moment to shine. I flicked on the charm, and made my way towards them with a selection of new words I'd been armed with that morning.

"Bonjour Mesdames" – starting on the right foot, giving them respectful titles like the well-raised gentleman that I am.

"Je suis perdu" – I'm lost. Laying my cards on the table. Making them aware that I'm a vulnerable foreigner in a strange land, and that this could be their day to be heroes.

"Quel est la meilleure route à Compiègne?" – What's the best road to take? Meilleure is a brilliant word. Great, great fun to say as well.

Just say the word 'MAYOR' with a really flamboyant, clipped English accent and you've nailed it.

"Merci beaucoup pour votre gentillesse." – Thank you for your kindness. Lovely parting shot, as was plain to see by their glowing smiles.

I had completely cast a spell over them with my linguistic skills. I stood quietly hoping they would give an answer consisting of extremely clear directions, preferably in English, so I wouldn't have to blow my cover and admit that I'd used all four of the French sentences I knew for this particular scenario.

Being typical old ladies, they disagreed with each other over which way to send me. I thought I'd let them squabble, while I nodded and pretended to have a clue about the finer points of their discussion. Finally, the bossier one took charge and pointed confidently in the direction of the second road on the right. They wished me well on my travels and mentioned that my French was "très bien", which absolutely made my day. Sylvie would have been proud. I took them at their word and pedalled along the road they'd signalled towards, with their crowing voices screeching "Au revoir! Bon voyage!" in unison as I went. Bless them. It was probably the most excitement they'd had in weeks.

Three further hours of scrapping through stubborn crosswinds came and went, as I tried doggedly to make it one mile at a time through the barren countryside. The vivid red bricks of Saint-Just-en-Chausée were the site of my final caffeine hit before putting the hammer down for the last twenty miles to make the B&B just outside Compiègne before darkness beat me to it.

A two-mile flyover bridge carried me across the murky waters of the Oise and Aisne rivers as daylight trickled away. I rolled onto Choisy-au-Bac's stone-covered streets, and propped my bike against the church fence to check directions on my map. From what I had scribbled on an old supermarket receipt that morning, I felt confident this was the street I was looking for. All I had to do now was locate the B&B, which had apparently been converted from an old 19th-century schoolhouse, run by a group of nuns. The schoolhouse that is, not the B&B. I wasn't in any fit state to spend my evening enduring solitude, silence and stale bread. Unclipping my helmet strap, I pushed my bike along the deserted road, when a sheepish voice unexpectedly called out from a doorway on the other side of the street.

"Bonjour Steve!"

There he was. The boy only went and did it.

Spence, you old dog.

"Two thousand miles? Why not do it over five years, and take your time to enjoy it!"

Antoine, owner of the renovated schoolhouse, didn't understand.

"My wife and I love cycling too. But we ride for three or four hundred miles each summer, and then start again the following year where we left off."

"I don't have that luxury, Antoine," I replied. "I have to be in Nice in ten days time."

"But you'll have no time to appreciate the places you're going through. You're wasting a good holiday!"

"Don't worry," I said, reaching for another teaspoon of sugar to stir into my coffee. "There'll be plenty of time to enjoy myself when I reach the south coast."

"You must have really strong bikes for all that luggage," said Antoine's wife, Ana-Livia, as she offered Spence another piece of Nutella-coated baguette.

"Funny, I only bought mine the day before starting this trip," I continued, with Spence otherwise occupied filling his face. "Little second-hand aluminium road bike. Not the touring bike you'd usually cart pannier bags around on, but it seems to be doing the job so far."

In fact, if my parents hadn't suggested the idea of purchasing a more robust set of wheels the day before my Grand Départ, I would genuinely have gone ahead and used my much-loved carbon bike from home. Which realistically would have got me as far as Lisburn before snapping in half under the creaking weight of all my gear. As I've already mentioned, foresight is not one of my fortés. I need sensible people around me.

I turned around and Spence was now face-first in a bowl of Nesquik.

We stayed up late teaching Ana-Livia and Antoine a selection of Northern Ireland songs on their grand piano, and listening to them tell us more details about their own two-wheeled quest – bit by bit along the length of the River Rhone. I loved that I wasn't the only one in the room who saw the thrill in setting unusual long-distance challenges. The primary reason they weren't doing it in one go, as far as I could see, was the fact that they have young children (who I imagine make month-long bike trips a bit tricky). And because they didn't need to, without the unerring passion for a football team driving them on. But apart from that, we were kindred spirits. Cut from the same adventure-hungry cloth.

After educating Spence in fine French cuisine the following morning with a taster menu of Orangina and brioche in Meaux, we pressed on through Coulommiers to the lesser known villages of Jouy-en-Chatel and Saint-Just-en-Brie. One goal I had set myself before arriving on foreign soil was to explore as much of the unseen France as possible. It's the same across the world I'm sure, but rugged gems are just waiting to be unearthed once you take a sideways turn off the beaten track. These are the places where you get to see the real essence of a country. Where you come face to face with farmers who work sixteen hours a day and wouldn't entertain the thought of a day off, bakers who not only know the names of every customer but all the other people in their village too, and families who stand outside their front door and offer you something to eat or drink if you hop off your bike for more than two minutes.

Having taken turns to shield each other from wild winds all day, even our boisterous renditions of 'From Paris down to Nice, being chased by the police' (Spence's inspired remix of school disco classic *'From Paris to Berlin'*) were beginning to lose some of their gusto. A slightly more prominent town called Maison Rouge soon appeared ahead of us, notable in that it didn't just consist of a town hall ("mairie"), boules area and church. Which is more than can be said for 90% of the villages in France. We dismounted, removed the buffs from our mud-speckled faces, and stepped into the town's solitary café.

"Is it OK if we bring our bikes in?" I asked as we clip-clopped over the tiles in our cleats.

The café had the appearance of a dusty American diner, with faded baseball photos and garish neon lights on the walls, and looked like it hadn't had a customer for decades. A balding middle-aged man slowly emerged from the gloom, like a contestant stepping onto the stage on Stars in Their Eyes.

"Hahahahaha. Non!" his voice boomed.

A smile broke out across my face as I lifted my head to look back at him. I'd missed this kind of sarcastic humour that we're so familiar with back home.

"So, where's the best place to put them? Is against this wall OK?"

"Non. You can *not* bring zem in. Zis is not a garage."

Turns out he was being serious. Spence and I shuffled back outside with our mugs of hot chocolate (actually, that's being kind to Monsieur Moodswing, it was more like tepid chocolate – and had probably now been laced with something), and we stood shivering at the wonky chest-high table situated a metre from the main road, as passing cars sprayed lying water in our direction.

The last twenty-five kilometres each day were always the easiest by far. You look at the roadsigns, divide by eight and multiply by five in your head, and realise there are only fifteen short miles to go. You start thinking of the first things you're going to eat when you stop, and by the time you've thought of that only twelve miles remain. You look down at your map and make a quick mental plan of the roads you'll need to navigate to reach your destination – all the while your legs keep spinning and the sign now says eight kilometres. Five miles. You're breezing along. The search for accommodation then becomes a treasure hunt, and pain and lethargy temporarily lift from your legs.

And then it's all over.

Coo-ey? Coy? Quee? Still none the wiser...

A cup of strong coffee and a couple of slices of pizza at Abdel's had put our latest exertion long behind us. Tucked away in a miniscule, unpronounceable village called Cuy (nope, not a clue either), it felt like we'd secured deal of the century in only paying thirty quid each for a night at his luxurious gaff. And the more time we spent in his company, the more of a cult hero he became in my eyes.

His howls of laughter increased in volume every time he pressed repeat on the video.

"Look! Look, he's climbing on to the table! He's going to fall! And this was just for qualifying, yes?"

On the night of Northern Ireland's momentous victory over Greece (the one that sealed our place at Euro 2016) a whole host of jubilant fan videos were shared online. The YouTube clip that Abdel was now fixated on had been taken inside a popular Belfast watering-hole heaving with hundreds of supporters, with the match beamed onto a vast projector screen in the distance. The final whistle blew, and mass hysteria erupted. Plastic pint glasses were launched from all angles, creating a cascade of golden liquid falling from the sky. Limbs flailed under spotlights in the euphoric crowd, complete strangers hugged and kissed one another, animated shrieks pierced through the wall of noise, and half a dozen revellers leapt on to the bar to perform some of the greatest dance moves seen since Thriller-era Michael Jackson.

I tried to imagine what it must look like through the eyes of a French fan (with both a World Cup and European Championship title in the past twenty years – not to mention their latest triumph in 2018) and watched his surprise, bordering on disbelief, that a group of supporters would celebrate so raucously an achievement that is the very, very least he expects from his own team.

His love of football aside, Abdel was a fascinating, eccentric character. Largely because we didn't know he existed before we arrived at his house. His online profile showed a picture of a beautiful lady called Sarah. She sent us texts and emails prior to arrival, but we only met her 'husband' Abdel when we got there. Sarah was either looking after their child, or in the bathroom, or at the shops, or preparing food in the kitchen on each of the occasions we asked.

Let's not fluff around the facts – Abdel had taken a picture from a magazine of an attractive female, and used it to lure young men to pay high prices at his B&B. Mind you, if that's what he had done, it had worked on us.

Gathering around a dinner table eating pizza lovingly handmade by "Sarah", it felt like I was explaining Northern Ireland's Euro 2016 squad as much to Spence as I was to Abdel. I did my utmost to articulate how difficult our prospective opponents were to them – one Frenchman who wasn't able to name anywhere in Northern Ireland except Dublin, and one Northern Irish man who was more interested in the type of cheese on his pizza than anything I had to say about Shane Ferguson's turn of pace.

"Hahahaaa! Who is that old man playing in goals for you? Is this some sort of family photo? Of him and his ten children?" chuckled Abdel, pointing at Roy Carroll in a team photo on his iPad.

(Roy, if you're reading this, his words not mine. You don't look a day over twenty-one.)

We had arrived at this illustrious abode after my third 100-miler in a row, and Spence's first day on the road by my side (or, to be more accurate, in front of me while I shamelessly stole his slipstream). It was a strange luxury having someone to chat to on the bike, let alone someone who spoke English and didn't require me to slow my rate of speech to two words a minute to make me out. When he stayed with me, that is.

Some of us hadn't just arrived fresh off a plane, and more than an ounce or two of fatigue was setting into my legs. I found myself yelling into the wind throughout the day for Spence to slow down, as time and time again he disappeared into the horizon like a greyhound each time I took my foot off the gas for a second through the wheat fields heading eastwards from Compiègne.

"Have you cycled from Ireland as well?" Abdel asked looking in the direction of Spence.

"No, this is my first day. I flew to Paris to join Steve."

"You're a cheat!" said Abdel abruptly.

Spence looked at me, not sure how to respond. I looked back, shrugged my shoulders and tried desperately hard not to cry with laughter.

"I bet you're going to jump on a train tomorrow," continued Abdel. He was just getting into his stride. "Do you even know how to cycle? You're probably going to fly home before he finishes too!"

He should probably have left it there, but Spence's honesty got the better of him.

"Yeah actually, I am. I'm flying home from Nice, and then Steve's heading on alone."

Abdel roared. I haven't seen someone laugh that hard in years. He wolfed down his final bite of pizza, and bounced out the door towards the kitchen to check on Sarah once more.

Even the most epic journeys need quiet days. And if they don't, they should. I like to imagine Sir Ed Hillary and Sherpa Tenzing having a couple of days on their way up Everest where they stayed in their sleeping bags all day, ate bacon butties and played Happy Families. I still had a massive number of miles to cover before Nice could even enter my thoughts and – despite what my chiselled, Hellenistic physique might suggest – my body is not a machine. Everyone needs rest.

Our "quiet day" involved a forty-five mile spin that took us into the magical old town atmosphere at the heart of Auxerre, where a young Eric Cantona started out on his professional football journey. I was fixated on Eric growing up as a Manchester United fan. The cocktail of his unpredictable, fiery temperament coupled with his majestic control of a football made him impossible for any Match of the Day addict in the mid-nineties to take their eyes off.

It's no coincidence that the most deeply loved sportspeople tend to be the ones who (accidentally or not) let their guard down from time to time, and give us a glimpse of who they really are without PR cover up. Nobody wants to support someone who's perfect. What hope does that give any of us? But when we can see bits of our own fragile selves behind the genius, that's when talented sportspeople (like Cantona, Zidane, Gascoigne and Best) become heroes. Because deep down, in many ways, they're just like one of us.

As we passed through Joigny en route to Auxerre, locals began to inform us that France was experiencing its heaviest rainfall for over fifty years, and that the water level of the sweeping Seine had risen to an all-time high. We quickly found the French equivalent of a greasy spoon and perched on the edges of plastic chairs outside the café to avoid sitting in the puddles collecting on the curved surface behind us.

"We're over half way for today already," said Spence, flicking through Google Maps while taking another bite of his increasingly soggy pizza.

"Shut up. You serious?"

"Twenty-five miles done, twenty to go. Decent sign when that only feels like a warm up".

Refuelling in Joigny with Spence on our "quiet" day

"That's ridiculous," I laughed. "We'll be done by the middle of the afternoon."

"Time to burn. Shall we?" asked Spence.

I nodded and smiled, as I turned and waved to the waitress inside.

That second main course didn't do me a button of harm as I cruised along the pancake-flat terrain approaching Auxerre after lunch. Spence, however, appeared to be suffering with the double whammy of pepperoni pizza that had just landed in his stomach. I've always been an advocate for eating whatever you like as long as you do a bit of exercise to clear the arteries – as my altogether better-cushioned exterior demonstrates.

"Carb loading!" I shouted over to Spence, gathering speed and overtaking him on a downhill stretch. "It's good for you, trust me." He looked up at me swallowing slowly and deliberately while his face turned an ashen grey, and fought with every ounce of his being to make sure neither of us saw that extra pizza again.

The bike really is a brilliant invention. Stop for a moment and think of life before bikes. Wheels had been doing the rounds for a while (no pun intended) and out of nowhere in the 19th century some Italian wannabe appeared saying that you should sit on a seat perched above two really narrow ones and keep pedalling continually because if you stop you'll fall off. "Ehh great idea mate. So, you're telling me if I want to go slightly faster than walking pace but not quite as fast as my horse and cart, I can hop onto your impossible two-wheeled contraption and arrive at my destination covered in sweat. Yeah, good luck with that." The dismissive roars of laughter would have been deafening.

It amazes me when I see a ten year old gliding along a pavement on a hoverboard or stacking twenty-one plastic cups into a pyramid in less than a second. These are things I can't do (and will never be able to do), because I didn't grow up doing them. That's the thing though. Most people *can* cycle, because it's still – by and large – seen as a rite of passage in the process of growing up.

You master the walker, then the tricycle, then the bike with stabilisers, then your first real bike (which if you were anything like me, was luminous green all over with lightning bolt stickers and 'MEAN MACHINE' emblazoned in capital letters across the frame).

It makes you wonder. What else could the next generation master if we taught it from an early age? What if every child was made to learn how to walk on their hands to get around? Or if all primary school teachers taught their pupils to master the art of tuned percussion instead of the recorder? That would add a bit of spice to end-of-year concerts. "Thank you Jack for chiming the tubular bells so beautifully to open tonight's proceedings. Now it's over to Lisa from P4 playing an ABBA medley on the marimba."

Far too many people appear obsessed with sucking the fun out of cycling. They initially embrace the thrill of careering through mountain passes and along rugged, coastal roads on two wheels. But before they're even aware they're doing it, they've bought one of those daft pointed helmets, conned themselves into believing that figure-hugging lycra looks great on them, and started answering the question "How was your cycle today, darling?" with a summary of their maximum watt output and miles per hour average.

You know someone's in too deep when cycling chat crops up everywhere, as they shoehorn information about their new bike's weight or their latest hill climb into the most unrelated conversation. They turn the sport into a yawn-inducing, exacting science where they're more preoccupied with exposing the Ironman tattoo on their hairy backs or trying to impress strangers in their office with Strava segments than simply phoning a mate, grabbing the bike from the garage, shoving a banana in their back pocket and taking in the buzz of cycling for a couple of hours as the sun sets just because they can.

There's no reason it can't be like that.

You don't have to cycle fast. At least not to start with. Five short miles to visit a relative on the other side of town, or to pick up a couple of litres of milk for your Coco Pops, can leave you feeling ten thousand times more alive and ready for the world when you return. But there lies the problem. In a world where we don't need to leave our front doors for work, entertainment or even shopping, the attitude of 'couldn't be bothered' is depressingly common.

Yet despite this laziness, we love watching other people do non-lazy things. We'll log onto Instagram on our phones and scroll endlessly through heavily-filtered images of friends going climbing in the Alps or long-lost-cousins twice-removed swimming with dolphins off the Australian coast or the twentieth mate from uni who's cycling from John O'Groats to Land's End for charity. All the while we're sprawled out like a beached octopus on our sofa scoffing down a family pack of Maltesers and complaining because we can't reach the TV remote and Tipping Point is about to start.

We love looking at pictures like these, because it reminds us there's a stunning world beyond our smartphones. Vast swathes of people might never venture into that world, but they find it comforting to know that a handful of people like David Attenborough and some of their more daring friends are willing to brave the elements and take breathtaking images so they can stay inside and just watch.

Who knows what might happen if they tried these adventures for themselves? After all, it's very hard to achieve anything in life if you never leave your comfort zone.

"Spence, pull over!" I shouted up ahead.

The noise of metal grinding against the tarmac had crescendoed until finally making itself heard above the whistling of the wind.

"The back tyre's gone. I'm gonna have to change it, sorry."

I freewheeled to a halt, and steered my bike into the unruly grass alongside the uphill stretch leading towards our B&B, which was no more than six miles from the city centre.

My cavalier approach to timekeeping had meant we'd spent all afternoon in Auxerre dipping in and out of bakeries, dancing with troupes of African street musicians, and postulating Will Grigg as a 21st-century Cantona to any locals who were willing to listen.

It had gone half past six when I packed the DIY teaspoons away once more, and we were back in the saddle. Although, only ten seconds later, came the most dreaded noise you can hear on a bike.

"You have got to be KIDDING me!" I yelled at the top of my voice.

"What's up now?" asked Spence, weariness in his voice. "Not another one, is it?"

The explosive nature of the sound told me that it was much worse than just another puncture. This was a full-scale blow-out. Same wheel that I'd replaced two minutes earlier too. The only problem this time was that the force of the puncture had blown a gaping tear in not just the inner tube, but the tyre itself. Ask any touring cyclist for a replacement inner tube and they'll offer you a handful (I was no different), but nobody carries spare tyres on them.

"Spence, what do I do?"

We were three miles out of the city and three miles from our destination. Well over an hour's walk in either direction pushing a bike loaded with pannier bags. And even at that, it wouldn't help us much waking up the following morning – on a Sunday when the country's shops shut down – still without a back tyre.

My internal interrogation began. Why didn't I take more care replacing that inner tube? Why hadn't I wasted less time in Auxerre and kept moving while places were open that could have fixed this mess? And if I had to improvise, could I stuff my unusable tyre with some of this grass from the roadside to carry me home? Does that even work? I remember reading a cycling magazine once that said you could do that as a last resort and bobble along for a few miles.

I instinctively did what I always do during times of crisis, and reached for a flapjack.

"Would it do *that much* damage if you just cycled the last few miles on the rims?" asked Spence, struggling to hold his eyes open against the wind whipping around us.

"What if you gave me a backie the rest of the way?"

"And your bike would go where exactly?"

"I could drag it along beside us, as long as you go slow enough."

"And your panniers?"

"I could carry them."

"At the same time as holding on to your bike? Face it Steve, this is rubbish. We might as well get our walking boots on."

I had another curious glance at the clump of grass brushing against my legs, when a silver car pulled on to the rocky hard shoulder on the opposite side of the road. Out stepped a slender, dark-haired lady whose shout was barely audible over the rushing traffic separating us from her.

"Ça va?"

At that moment I broke every rule of polite British social convention and did not respond by saying that I was fine.

"Non! Mon vélo est fini!" I said, emphasising the point by throwing my hands up to represent the tyre exploding. She looked baffled by my impromptu interpretative dance, but continued to speak, saying something very fast and very French.

She soon realised she was speaking to two foreigners more likely to recite the entire unabridged works of Shakespeare than string together a coherent sentence in French, and begun asking us about our predicament in broken English. After a few minutes, she signalled with her hand and said "Attends!" ("Wait!") before turning her back and taking out her mobile phone.

Five minutes later, she returned to invite me to hop into her car and race back to Auxerre with my dodgy tyre, while Spence sat on the roadside and watched over the two bikes. With my phone battery dead at the time, I only realised later how vulnerable this left Spence. Sitting in the dirt at the edge of a busy road in a country he didn't know, without the address for the place we were booked to stay at, and with no means of contacting me – just hoping that the complete stranger who had whisked me away might return at some unspecified point in the near future.

Claire – the name of our unlikely heroine – turned to me on the drive towards the city and admitted with a look of disbelief and mild apprehension on her face, "I've never given a man I don't know a lift in my car before. Never. I can't believe I'm doing this, but I just felt like you needed help."

It turned out she had a close friend who owned the only bike shop that was still open in Auxerre, and even it was due to close at 7pm. That left us two minutes to make it. She dialled this friend's number on her hands-free as we drove, and asked him to keep the shutters open a few minutes longer.

French bike shops are like nothing you've ever experienced. You might think your standard UK-based Halfords handyman with a few road bikes hanging from his wall knows his stuff, but it's a whole different level in France. It's so engrained in who they are. Think of all the words that cyclists use – peloton, soigneur, domestique, derailleur – everything about the sport is steeped in French culture. It's their sport. And my word, their bike mechanics know what they're playing at.

One glance to check for size, and Claire's mate had a new tyre over my weary, old wheel – using his grimy bare hands for everything (not a tyre lever or teaspoon in sight) – in less than a minute. For a ham-fisted wannabe like me, it was phenomenal to witness. I threw him fifteen euros for his trouble, and Claire whisked me back to a shivering Spence out in no-mans-land. In my absence, Spence had looked up contact details for our accommodation online, and our B&B hosts had arrived with a trailer in tow.

Loading the trailer for the final stretch home after Claire's heroics

Having strapped the bikes in, we thanked Claire for her kindness and asked her to apologise to her children for stopping them getting a lift home from swimming lessons. We said our goodbyes, before being chauffeured the final three miles to a stately home tucked away in the most remote countryside.

We stayed in a castle that night. If it hadn't been for Claire we would have been sleeping in a desolate roadside ditch. Ernest Hemingway once said "As you get older it is harder to have heroes, but it's sort of necessary." Stranded on that gloomy hard shoulder, with my dream of reaching Nice evaporating in front of my eyes, Claire was *absolutely* necessary and to this day remains a hero.

Pain had by now become a daily visitor to my legs.

The first hour of each new morning was spent enduring agonising joint pain, before steadily but surely pedalling it out of my system. Until it returned the following morning, that is. Swinging my legs out of bed was a real chore. Standing up from the toilet seat now felt worryingly difficult. I was only eight days in, and I already felt like I'd adopted the knee joints of a severely arthritic 90-year-old man.

In our castle the night before, I had followed proceedings via my phone (and cost myself a small fortune in mobile data) as Northern Ireland played their final friendly match before the journey across to join us in France. A drab goalless draw against Slovakia wasn't exactly a thrill-a-minute as I read the on-screen updates from the live feed, but new boy Conor Washington impressed, Aaron Hughes collected his 100th cap – becoming the first outfield NI player in history to do so – and the result ensured we would strut into our first match at Euro 2016 on the back of a twelve-game unbeaten streak.

It was an unusually mild Sunday morning, as Spence and I crossed a stone bridge over the tranquil river running through Vincelottes, and soon stumbled upon a colourful blur of weekend activity in the wine-producing town of Irancy. Tucked in the hollow of a valley, this unassuming rural community are famous for their red wines.

So I'm told at least. Not that we stopped to sample them at nine in the morning.

As we freewheeled through its streets, we waved at a group of six cyclists who were passing round a flask of coffee before their own morning spin. Children played with skipping ropes and tricycles outside their houses, as parents stood and watched from their doorways eating croissants and catching up with next-door neighbours.

"Shame those cyclists are going the other way," I turned and said to Spence.

"Yeah, especially with this beast of a climb coming up."

I glanced ahead at the seemingly never-ending ascent to the summit reached only via winding roads through the vineyards, and puffed out my chest. "It has to be done. Anyway, it'll be good practice ahead of the Alps."

"You take the lead for the first bit" said Spence. "We'll swap after a few corners."

I flicked down my gears as low as they would allow, and started grinding up the incline coming off the first bend. I'd only got a couple of hundred metres when I heard an almighty crunch behind me.

"No!" yelled Spence, "What is your problem?"

I couldn't think of anything I'd done to annoy him that much. It was only when I looked over my shoulder that I realised he was talking to his bike.

"Useless piece of crap!" he went on. "Why are you doing this to me?"

It might have been best to let Spence and the bike settle this one between themselves, but I eventually chose to descend and see if I might be able to act as mediator.

"What's all this about?" I asked.

"I don't know. I don't even care anymore. The back thing's hanging off."

Spence's derailleur – the unruly mesh of metalwork responsible for gear shifting – had cracked down the middle, and was now dangling pathetically near his ankles.

"How are we supposed to fix that?" said Spence, scratching his bushy mop of hair, his eyes locked on the broken 'back thing' and a shell-shocked glare on his face.

"I could cycle back to Auxerre and find that shop from last night."

"It's Sunday," mumbled Spence forlornly. "Nowhere's gonna be open."

He was right. The country was in complete lockdown. I left Spence surveying his mechanical devastation under a tree and nipped back into Irancy to recruit whatever help I could find. When I got there, every shop and restaurant and bar was closed. Thinking frantically as I pedalled, I darted towards the kitchen on the corner where the group of cyclists had congregated minutes before. Sadly the green, wooden door was now bolted shut and they were nowhere to be seen.

A young father pushing his son on a toy tractor came into view on the other side of the street. I scurried across and described Spence's dilemma to him, with lots of actions to cover up the gaps in my vocab. His son seemed to find it funny at least. This affable gent then proceeded to explain the intriguing concept of the late weekend in France – that everywhere shuts not only on Sundays but also on Mondays, to allow traders an extra day's break following normal opening hours on Saturdays. I decided to keep this gem of cultural knowledge to myself, as sharing this info with Spence may well have precipitated a full-blown emotional meltdown.

While I'd been away searching for locals, Spence had mustered up the energy to clamber from his despondent perch under the tree, and had subsequently found a new friend of his own. I caught sight of the white frame of his bike being lifted through the door of a terraced house, and went over to find out more. I knocked on the open door, before taking a hesitant step inside.

"Bonjour?" I bellowed optimistically.

Nobody answered.

No people, anyway. A few seconds later, a boisterous golden labrador sprung down the hallway and leapt at me, placing its front paws firmly on my chest. Maybe this dog was a bike-obsessed, man-eating monster that had devoured Spence and dragged his broken bicycle into its lair. I couldn't tell for sure.

In the middle of being licked half to death, Pascal suddenly appeared from the dark shadows of his kitchen at the rear of the house.

"You must be Stephen?" he asked.

I nodded, turning my head and trying to keep my lips tightly sealed to avoid getting a mouthful of dog tongue.

"Come in, we're having a look at your friend's bike in the garage."

Having only done around five miles before the incident, I didn't really feel like I'd earned a break, but I wasn't going to say no when Pascal placed a steaming mug of coffee and a bag of Madeleines on the kitchen table in front of me.

If I had to rank all the baked goods on offer in France in a league table, Madeleines would probably come a close second just behind the peerless brioche. Pain aux raisins could make a decent case for third spot. Brioche is the daddy – especially when it comes in loaf form – but Madeleines are sensational, and they are prime cycling food. An average bag contains around thirty cakes and they're tough to beat when you've got a case of the munchies during a long day in the saddle.

Spence and Pascal had reached the unfortunate conclusion that a specialist was needed to provide the relevant bike parts, and a decent shop was the only answer. News about Monday opening hours had now filtered through to Spence, but he decided he'd take a gamble and get a train to wherever I told him to aim for, and hope he could locate somewhere on arrival.

My bike – still in working order – sat outside chained to the gate in the town square where it had been for over two hours. It was almost midday, and I had 150km to cycle if I was going to make my planned destination of Beaune by evening. Surely that wasn't going to be possible now.

Spence and Pascal both stared in my direction, waiting for a decision. I reached for another Madeleine. I was delaying the inevitable. I knew what I had to do. Pushing my seat out from under the kitchen table, I thanked Pascal for breakfast and stepped through his front door back onto the street.

Giving Spence a manly pat on the back, I flashed a wry grin and said "If I never see you again, it's been good fun," before unlocking my bike, looking ahead and beginning the excruciating scramble up that hill of vineyards once more.

By now, friends back home in Northern Ireland had started sending me text messages telling me that they'd heard me on the radio in the hairdressers or the supermarket or the chemist. I loved the thought of old ladies sitting silently for their weekly perm listening to me giving an interview about my saddle sores or the most unique places I'd emptied my bowels recently.

My closest brush with fame up to this point in my life had either been winning second prize for handwriting at the Lurgan Show as a five-year old, or breaking the world record for wrapping someone head to toe in newspaper live on university radio. Three minutes and five seconds, in case you're wondering. No scissors allowed. This was different though. Almost every day, a link to another article emerged in my email inbox featuring a sweaty, purple-faced picture of me on my bike.

As oddly exciting as this was, the biggest buzz for me was flopping into bed each night and reading comments from followers on social media. Schoolmates I hadn't heard from in over a decade, cycling enthusiasts I'd never met, and Northern Ireland fans who'd learnt about my trip through their supporters clubs. Word was spreading. Far further than I could grasp while trapped in my little bubble on that bike seat for ten hours each day.

High above the vineyards, I stopped to regain my breath. Squinting slightly as the wind swelled again, I could just about make out the tiny speck that was Pascal's house in the valley beneath me. I had now returned to the world of massive, exposed grassy plains, with only the odd rusty water tower to break up the landscape. Howling crosswinds threatened to throw me from my bike – who a friend from home had now christened Finn, with it being a 'Giant' (in bike branding terms at least) and hailing from the North Coast of Ireland, just like Mr MacCool – as I pedalled onwards. Singing, as ever, remained my primary form of therapy.

Sweet Caroline (in full, all three verses and chorus to fade) was rolled out at least ten times that afternoon, my eyes watering from the wind chill and my cries of "So good, so good, so good" reverberating through the vast, sweeping countryside.

Nitry and Noyers were ticked off early on, before I took late lunch in the medieval village of Châtel-Gérard with its no more than three hundred inhabitants. There aren't any substantial towns between Auxerre and Beaune, meaning my solitary Sunday involved lots of Sunday-speed countryside cycling into Sunday-level traffic (absolutely nothing) through immaculately-kept villages engaging in Sunday-like behaviour (doing very little). There weren't exactly street carnivals taking place everywhere I went. It was a day for blasting out extra miles while the world around me slept.

On long, unaccompanied days in the saddle, you craft your own entertainment. I never felt lonely. I adored the freedom. Nobody to get frustrated at my tendency to take things too slowly or the way I never ever make plans. Living for the moment with nothing else to clutter or preoccupy your thoughts. When you're sailing through a timid village in some long-forgotten corner of France, even the smallest things grab your attention.

You notice tantalising smells drifting through gaps in kitchen windows and detect glimpses of sarcastic humour as locals greet one another. You pick out tunes that church bells are playing and spot idyllic red-roofed houses high on the sides of mountains. It makes you feel like a three-year old again. Getting excited at seeing and experiencing things just because they're there.

We hardly even see outside the walls of our houses. We wake up to go to work before coming home and closing ourselves away. I read a few years back that the vast majority of people in London don't set foot on grass at any point in the average week. And that children were three times more likely to injure themselves falling out of bed than falling out of a tree. But then I thought about myself – the boisterous, active explorer I like to see myself as – and realised that for the majority of my working life all of that's been just as true for me. Especially the falling out of bed bit.

There's nothing boring about cycling on your own. It can *definitely* be exhausting, lung-busting, painful, frightening, cold and mentally-draining (amongst many other things). But it's never boring.

As afternoon became evening, Pouilly-en-Auxois and Colombier now long behind me, I started to wonder how Spence and his broken bike were getting on. Just before I left him that morning we had discovered news of a nationwide train strike, meaning significantly decreased services. I wasn't concerned that he'd struggle to find transport. There were lines still running, even if it wasn't the most direct route. I did, however, have a new challenge to drive me on. Could I make it to Beaune on two wheels faster than Spence could on a high-speed train?

Beaune lay in a valley beyond a considerable mound in the landscape, otherwise known as Beaune Mountain. My legs weren't exactly having the time of their lives as I remained stood out of my saddle throughout the fight to reach the summit. Boxed in by trees most of the way, there wasn't much to look at. Just me and my little early-evening chamber of pain. Sunlight was fading rapidly and – although I definitely hadn't planned it – I was treated to the most amazing sunset the very moment I arrived at the peak. With the sun having just dropped over the horizon behind me, the sky was painted with broad brushstrokes of purples and oranges.

I flicked my feeble back light into action and steamed down the other side of the mountain. There isn't much that's as exhilarating as tearing down a steep descent on two wheels. Hitting 50mph on a road bike gives a burst of adrenaline that's very hard to replicate in any other sport. Streetlights were the only things lighting my path by the time I swept on to the wide, brown-tiled streets of Beaune's walled city.

Christian and Marie, a married couple in their late 60's, locked my bike in their garage and welcomed me in. A range of fresh breads, orange juice and chocolate lay waiting for me in the kitchen, which we tucked into together. And most importantly, there was no Spence yet. I'd done it. A momentous achievement for the human race in our struggle against machinery. My phone started ringing, and it was the man of the moment saying he'd be landing at the train station in just under an hour. He sounded thoroughly fed up. I felt like an absolute champion, and poured myself some more O.J. to toast my victory.

Pulling up at the train station, it didn't take long for us to spot the forlorn, slightly moody individual sitting on the cold steps still cradling his broken bicycle in his arms.

"Allow me to help you," offered Christian, as he took hold of the bike and positioned it into his car boot, trying to slam the door shut behind it.

"Stop! What do you think you're playing at?!" shrieked Spence. "You're going to break it even more! Let me do it."

Christian took a step back, bemused. It was clear that somebody's stress levels had remained ever so slightly elevated since earlier.

On returning to the house, Spence carefully lifted his baby into the garage, while I returned to the kitchen and tried to patch things up with poor, shell-shocked Christian. He sat deep in thought, probably wondering what reprobates he'd just allowed into his home. Two cups of tea and a bar of Milka later, and thankfully our conflict resolution talks had come to a peaceful conclusion.

After a night to sleep on things, Spence bounced out of bed a new man. He apologised to Christian for his icy attempt at first impressions, and they joked over breakfast as though nothing untoward had happened. Disappointingly, Beaune had nothing to offer in the way of bike repair, and Spence came to realise that he would most likely have to consign himself to another day out of action. Twenty-four more hours without even the slightest hint of leg pain, back pain or perineal pain (to use the correct medical terminology).

Pedalling off by myself into the overcast heat of the day once more, my heart didn't exactly bleed for him.

As ever, time was working against me. Evenings on the road were never relaxing.

The typical morning start, with twelve hours spread like an ocean in front of me, meant I would set out meandering slowly from village to village with no sense of urgency whatsoever. Not a care in the world. By lunchtime, I would reassess and normally realise that I needed to turn the pedals slightly faster to keep me roughly on track. Then by the time the afternoon was out and evening set in, without exception, I would end up blowing out of my hoop and pedalling like wildfire to try and reach my accommodation before darkness engulfed me and I was lost forever.

It looked like I'd just about got away with it again. Yes, I'd cut it extremely fine, but as the sun dipped beneath the horizon I noticed the red-bordered road sign for Challes – the place I'd arranged to stay. Spence had been forced to hastily book a hotel in a far-off city, after predictably finding nowhere to get his bike fixed. Another lonesome night in the sticks lay in store for me. I pulled out my phone to check the address I was searching for, but none of the directions or road names seemed to correlate with what I saw around me.

As I tried to make some sense of Google Maps, my phone began to ring. It was an unrecognised number. I picked up and a French lady, in shaky but mostly understandable English, began to speak.

"Ello. Is zat you?"

"Hi, yeah, it's Stephen. Nice to hear from you. I'm in Challes. Just trying to find your house now."

"Oh zat is very well. Great. Where har you at zis moment?"

"I'm somewhere in Challes, I know that much. To be honest, it all just looks like fields."

"You have field wiv you? Zat is strange. I can not zink of any field in Challes. Har you diffinitely in Challes at zee meenit?"

"Yes, there's a big sign saying Challes beside me, and a load of fields. Fields everywhere. Can you describe your house?"

"My ouse is very nice. Eet is zee biggest ouse on ze mountain top. Eet has a red roof and a beeg garage door. When you harrive in Challes la Montagne, eet is the first zing you see."

Hold. The. Phone.

As my host continued to rattle on in her peculiar voice, my eyes darted across the map and saw another village fifteen miles to the east, called Challes la Montagne. A bead of sweat trickled down one side of my face.

Nobody said there were two Challes. And it wasn't just fifteen miles that separated them, but also three mountains. Fan-flipping-tastic.

"Ok, it turns out I'm not actually in your village."

"But ow? You have been saying zat you were here."

"I'm fifteen miles away. I'm in the wrong Challes."

"Oh non, not zat Challes! Oh dear you har funny."

I wasn't trying to be, love.

The moment I put down the phone after hearing I was in the wrong Challes

It was after nine o'clock and I still had – at the very least – an hour and a half of cycling to go, punctuated by stretches of steep, unforgiving terrain for much of that distance. And having to complete the whole trek on weary legs in the faint glow of my slowly-dying bike lights just added an extra element of fun to the mix.

As this was the first time I'd needed to use both bike lights on the trip, it was also the first time I realised that I didn't have a holder for my front light. I tried to create an impromptu solution using a couple of cable ties from the random assortment of junk in my front pannier. These did a brilliant job of limply shining the light in the vague direction of my right foot, but not much else. I soon gave up and instead just held the light in one hand while trying to balance the bike with the other. All the more difficult when you're trying to stand up out of your seat to drive your hefty 80-plus kilogram backside up a small mountain.

It was punishing to reach, but when I eventually did get there her mountain-top chalet was a dream. Tiptoeing through the tassled, fabric door that brushed over my head as I entered the living room,

I slinked past a picnic-style dining table and up the stairs to the king-size bed in my room. Two chilled bottles of sparkling water sat perched beside the lamp on the bedside table. I don't even like sparkling water, but I celebrated my unpredictable, and at times unlikely, late-night arrival by glugging it like champagne.

Dominating one wall in my room, a brightly-coloured world map caught my attention. Pins had been placed on numerous locations from where previous guests had travelled. My eyes were drawn to Northern Ireland, which curiously had one pin already placed in it. Interesting, I thought. I wonder who's stumbled upon this secluded spot before me. Beside the pin, someone had written "Stephen from Coleraine". After standing with my glass of sparkling water and scratching my head for ten minutes trying to recall other Stephens I know from home, it clicked. It was my name. She'd been expecting me. Slightly presumptious considering the ordeal I'd been through in order to reach her, but a nice touch nonetheless.

Nine hours later, my eyes opened to the sound of a cockerel clearing his throat just below my window. Long after daybreak. Turns out even the poultry in France have a blasé approach to timekeeping. Shuffling down the creaking wooden stairs – I think it was the stairs, but it could have been my knees – I caught sight of a mouth-watering array of fruit and breads on the table, lit up by morning sun splitting through the curtains. A small, ruffled handwritten note lay beside the food saying "Sorry I'm not here to say goodbye but I have to go to work. Enjoy your breakfast!" I imagined her saying it in her comical French accent and chuckled. What a girl.

As I demolished another croissant dripping with chocolate spread, her husband appeared at the top of the staircase in his pyjamas. He worked nights as a lorry-driver, and had heard me sneaking past his door moments earlier. Rubbing his bleary eyes, he came and joined me for a bite of petit déjeuner. We talked about our shared loves of cycling and football and drank a couple of mugs of unnecessarily exotic herbal tea, before he requested that I taught him some typical Northern Irish greetings.

"What kind of greetings do you want to learn?" I asked.

"Ehhh, like, what can I say if I am to meet another man or lady from Irlande du Nord?"

"If you're greeting a friend, you'd start off by saying 'What's the craic?'"

"What?" he replied, confused and a little suspicious that I might be taking him for a ride. "Why are you talking about the crack? Where is the crack?"

"No, seriously. It's an old Irish word. Got nothing to do with drugs, honest. Over here, I guess you could say 'Quel est le craic?'"

Defining 'craic' is a conversation that all Northern or Southern Irish people will have had at some stage in their life with people unused to our unique ways. And the confusion only intensifies when you start explaining that "Craic is good fun" or "Dave's party was alright I suppose, but there wasn't much craic." Cue a sea of concerned faces all around. At this point, the normal response is for your polite overseas friends to ever-so-slowly reach for their mobile to bring in the local authorities.

We continued to bond while I slapped on my seventeenth layer of sun cream outside his front door. Yes, that's right. It had arrived. That unfamiliar, yellow thing in the sky that our ancient Greek ancestors once worshipped. The sun had remained a distant memory for me for the past eight days since it was last spotted somewhere over County Wexford. My skin had become so finely tuned to deflecting rainwater that I could tell I was going to be fried like an overdone kipper in the first few hours of this new day's cycling. The heat felt uncomfortable after only five minutes of standing in it. This was a very different kind of sunshine from Irish sunshine. The temperature was stifling, and I mopped snow-white beads of sweat from my brow as the suncream and my own perspiration blended into one and trickled from my forehead.

My trucker friend sat in the shade of a small palm tree and finished off the last of his verbena tea (I wouldn't bother – it tastes like a combination of ditchwater and what you spit into the sink after brushing your teeth). He looked at me through his over-sized sunglasses and kindly offered free accommodation for when I next visit, since Spence hadn't been able to take the place we'd paid for this time round. Mind you, if I ever did manage to scale that mountain again, I would expect more than just a free room for the night. I'd expect the Freedom of the Village. Or maybe they could just name their village after me, so nobody would get confused with its namesake down the road ever again. One Challes is more than enough for anyone.

I hunched my shoulders as I pedalled to try and stop the sun burning the skin on the back of my neck. From one extreme to the next. If it wasn't chucking it down sideways with rain, it was so searingly hot that all you wanted to do was run for cover. My second drinks refill of the day took place in Nantua, a bustling town lying at the end of the bluest of turquoise blue lakes. Sunbathing holidaymakers lay scattered upon sandy beaches around the edge of the lake, and ice-cream sellers grinned ear to ear from the roaring business they were doing. After a morning in the full glare of the sun, I avoided the lakeside fun and games and took shelter – and filled my bottles – inside a kebab shop. The temptation got the better of me while I was there (as it usually does), and I ordered a cheeky lamb doner for the road.

With most of my pre-lunch riding that day having involved gliding effortlessly downhill, I knew a time was coming soon where I'd pay for it. And almost as soon as I wheeled out of Nantua, the road started to creep in an upwards trajectory. Eyes fixed on the horizon as ever, I crawled along the road; the vast, vertical wall of rock towering above me to my right an early indication that we weren't far from entering the *real* mountains.

Cars flew past at breakneck speed. You always hear them long before you see them. I made a deliberate effort not to look at them as they revved their engines and sped past to avoid wobbling off course and landing face-first onto one of their bumpers.

After establishing something of a rhythm on one of the long, gradual climbs, I heard a car approaching but then didn't see it shoot past. How strange. I slowed down my pedalling and turned my head to the left, to see Spence creeping alongside me in his sleek, silver hire car. Raybans perched on his forehead and left arm hanging out of the window, he couldn't have rubbed it in more if he tried. Holding his cameraphone with one hand, he shouted "Allez allez allez, up up up!" like I was cycling through baying crowds on one of the mountain stages of the Tour de France.

"Did you get it fixed?" I called across, working hard to keep up with him.

"Yep all sorted! I'll be back on the road tomorrow." The stress that had been eating away at him had lifted. I suppose driving past your sweaty mate at 70mph would make you feel pretty good.

"Anyway, can't hang around. See you in Annecy, slowcoach!" he yelled with great gusto, as he waved and accelerated off into the distance.

My family's trailer tent cuts a sad and lonely figure in a garage these days, collecting sheets of dust as the months and years go by. In its heyday though, it allowed us to discover incredible pockets of France that we otherwise could only have dreamt of.

Camping gets an awful reputation. Lots of people bad-mouth it because of that Duke of Ed hike in their school days when they got horrendously lost or woke up with their sleeping bag in a puddle or when a badger nicked all their kitchen utensils and their last pack of Cadbury's Mini Rolls. But it teaches you about life in a way that a hotel or beach hut never will. Life can be messy and surprising, and camping gives you an education in how to deal with a whole host of tough stuff. And still, you're always glad you went.

Thinking back to my family's annual summer pilgrimage to France, the uncomfortable moments bring back the most vivid memories. Like getting locked out of campsites and having to slum it in the car. Or struggling to assemble our rusty tent frame in the dark while Dad lost his rag because we'd ignored his instructions again. Or my brother falling off his hired mountain bike at speed and slashing his thigh wide open (and bearing the angry scar to this day).

Experiences, like wild camping, that stretch you and teach you more about yourself and the world around you are much more rewarding in the long run. Some friends of mine refer to this as Category Two Fun. Stick with me while I explain.

Going to the cinema is Category One Fun. As is heading out for a nice meal, binge-watching shows on Netflix or buying a new car. Category One Fun is passive. You don't need to do anything in return for pleasure. It is fed to you. At the time, it feels brilliant. Like there's nothing in the world you'd rather be doing. No effort is required and, let's be fair, that's most people's idea of bliss.

On the flipside, Category Two Fun is not easy at the time. You need to use your initiative, and engage some physical and mental muscle. In fact, it's sometimes so tough that you'll feel like you want to give up. But by sticking at it and seeing it through, that new thing – whether it's climbing a mountain or learning how to paint, kayaking the length of a river or building a new garden shed – will give you far, far more pleasure in hindsight than Category One Fun ever will. Long-lasting satisfaction, that you've had to earn. And that's what makes camping great.

By far, the most memorable place we camped as a family was Annecy. Tucked by a beautiful, crystal-clear lake on the fringe of the French Alps, it is like being transported to a different world. The lake – the dramatic centrepiece around which local activity bustles – is framed by a border of rolling hills. In my teenage years, we spent one unforgettable summer after another pitching the trailer tent by Lake Annecy, filling long days in the sun leaping off the back of pedaloes into the clear water, tandem paragliding from Mount Semnoz, and cycling for hours on end along the purpose-built cycle paths.

Part of me was apprehensive about returning eleven years later. Things can feel smaller and less impressive when you return to somewhere you knew and loved in your younger days. I shouldn't have worried. Sheltered by thick white clouds for most of the day, the sun reared its head just as I crossed the final set of traffic lights bringing me onto the grassy park area at the town end of the lake.

The water stretched so far into the distance ahead of me, I could barely make out the shore on the opposite side. Annecy buzzed with life just like I remembered. A path cut through the middle of the park, with olive-skinned people on bikes and rollerblades shooting past at a rate of knots. I didn't know people even used rollerblades anymore. I hadn't seen a pair of those things for about fifteen years. Groups of joggers dashed by on training runs, couples held hands as they strolled along the waterfront, and there was barely a patch of grass free with the crowds gathered there.

As I cycled towards our campsite at the other end of the lake it felt like, if anything, the lake had got bigger with the passing of time. Having only cycled very small portions of the path around its perimeter as a youngster, I don't think I ever fully appreciated just how far this vast body of water stretches. Twelve kilometres later and still not halfway around, I met Spence on his own bike at the eco-village we'd booked to stay at for the night.

"When did you get here?" I asked, wondering why he'd appeared on two wheels and not four.

"About three hours ago. I've already done one and a half laps."

Testing out his reincarnated bike against the backdrop of the third largest lake in France had injected new life into Spence. He was fired up and ready to go. I was the opposite. Just about managing to turn my legs the required distance to slump into the boutique tent we'd been given at our hippy commune, I asked Spence if he'd kindly use some of that renewed energy and verve to go and buy a couple of croissants.

After an overnight stay with slugs crawling up the walls, and no running water or towels (because, you know, washing them might upset Mother Nature and kill orangutans and stuff), Spence abandoned his hire car at the local rental centre and we rejoined the cycle path with only one thought in our minds.

Time to aim for the mountains.

When I was eight I used to collect stickers with the faces of footballers on them, now I just take out my phone and follow them on Twitter.

Spence and I had pulled our bikes up to a café in the former Winter Olympic host city of Albertville and placed our orders. Accessing the complimentary wifi, I saw a handful of new notifications on Twitter. One of them was a message from Kyle Lafferty.

I remembered sending a small selection of messages to the NI players about my journey through France, but I wasn't expecting anything in reply. Surely this can't be real, I thought. It's got to be a random punter with the same name as the big man, or maybe someone with a fake account.

I looked further, and there was a blue tick underneath his profile picture. He had thousands of followers. Hang on, this is actually him. My heart pounded inside my chest. I needed to try and relax. I was starting to hyperventilate, and the bearded waiter at the café was showing signs of concern for my wellbeing.

I opened the message.

It simply read "Best wishes Steven on your bike ride" with a link attached to my fundraising page. Overlooking the fact that he had spelt my name wrong, I picked my lower jaw up off the table and retweeted it with more vigour than I'd ever retweeted a tweet in my life. Now I felt content that this was a legitimate way to spend a month. Kyle's seal of approval was all I needed. Spence spent the rest of lunch trying to calm me down, but I was a lost cause.

We wandered further into Albertville afterwards and the stamp left on the town by the Winter Olympics was plain to see. To think that the world's finest lugers, curlers and ski jumpers descended on this remote town in February 1992 is incredible, a place with a population the same as Larne. (Larne, for those not familiar, is an inconveniently out-of-the-way Northern Irish seaside town most well-known for the coastal road driving away from it and the boats leaving it.) Or to put it in context, Albertville's population of under 20,000 would fit into Stoke fifteen times over, or London 450 times. It has a big heart though. To use a term often thrown about in honour of the Northern Ireland football team, it's small but massive.

Several venues remain in use such as La Halle Olympique, featuring its original ice rink (which hosted the Olympic figure skating competition). The curling venue has been converted into a leisure centre and the outdoor speed skating venue (the last of its kind used at a Winter Olympics) has been given a new lease of life as a football stadium. On top of all that, the ski resorts used like Tignes, Les Arcs and Val d'Isère have gone on to become some of the most popular winter sports resorts in Europe. When so much bad press is given to the shoddy, short-sighted legacy left by Olympic host cities (not mentioning names, ahem, Athens and Atlanta), it was heartening to see a place use its Olympic badge of honour to such brilliant effect in making their little corner of the world more attractive and opportunity-rich for its inhabitants and the generations to come.

First glimpse of snow as we rolled into the Alps

Almost as soon as Albertville had disappeared out of the rear view mirror, droplets of rain began to land on our cheeks again. There seemed to be less traffic on the roads as we followed the most direct route into the heart of the mountains. At the same time, this heading into the mountains brought with it a wicked micro-climate of weather. But my mind had been made up. Two days previously, just before leaving Challes, I'd decided to crack on with the plan of going straight up and over the mountains to reach Nice. The inevitable torture of scaling a few Alpine mountains could have been replaced with an extra couple of hundred miles on the flat by looping inland. But where's the Category Two fun in that?

By the time several imposing mountains had started appearing either side of us, the rain was drumming down. Hailstones bounced off the road in front of us, and struck our helmets and the backs of our raincoats with such force that we couldn't even hear each other speak. This was fast turning into a heads-down sprint for home, with spray caking our faces in a speckled, brown mask as we took turns on the wheel of the person in front.

With twenty miles to go until our bed for the night, we were well and truly in time trial mode. Puffing and blowing and gasping for air, but unable and unwilling to stop due to the unrelenting storm and the dual carriageway we now found ourselves on.

"TEN MILES TO GO SPENCE!" I yelled up ahead, taking a mouthful of rainwater from Spence's back wheel for my trouble. Maybe it was mild delirium from the cold, but I'd switched into full-on, unhinged American football coach mode.

"YOU'RE LOOKING FANTASTIC, BUDDY! KEEP THE HAMMER DOWN!"

"WHAT?" came Spence's confused reply.

"I SAID…KEEP ON GOING! YOU'RE FLYING!"

"WHAT DO YOU MEAN I'M FINE?"

"NO, I SAID…AAAH FORGET IT. I'M COMING TO THE FRONT NOW!"

I waited for a gap in traffic, ramped up the revs and took over duties at the front. My face was now firmly fixed in that half-smile, half-grimace that I tend to do when I'm so physically drained that I'm entering the early stages of losing the will to live. Adrenaline was sustaining me though, and there was a weird, masochistic buzz from knowing we were ploughing headlong into the wild, cavernous mountains in front of us where the outlook was only going to getting more extreme.

A sign flashed by, indicating five miles to go before we could peel off the main road. My legs had become locked into a metronomic rhythm. I knew I couldn't keep this up forever. Yelling orders at myself in the midst of the wall of noise was all I could do to remind me that in half an hour it would all be over. Man up. Skin is waterproof. Be thankful you've got two legs. Keep pedalling you big mess. Did you really think cycling the length of France would be easy? Pull yourself together. Pain is weakness leaving the body. Keep driving and stop whining.

Just then, out of nowhere, the most awful screech, thud and scream pierced through the air.

"AAAAAHHHHHHHHHHHH!"

"SPENCE? NOT AGAIN! HANG ON!"

I slowed to a halt, and tucked in tight against the metal barriers at the side of the road. When I turned around, things didn't look too peachy.

Man down.

"DON'T WORRY SPENCE, I'M ON MY WAY!" I could hear the Baywatch music striking up inside my head as I sprinted (aka stumbled through puddles in my cleats like a high-heeled secretary trying to run after a bus) through the rain.

The poor soul was crumpled in a heap under his sorry bike, with one of his pannier bags lying two metres away in the middle of the road. Cars and vans veered wildly around him, as a stream of headlights continued to emerge through the mist.

I threw my bike against the barrier, and leapt to stand with my back to Spence directing high-speed traffic into the other lane with flailing arm actions that wouldn't have looked out of place on an airport runway.

"I HOPE YOU REALISE I'M RISKING MY LIFE FOR YOU HERE!" I shouted a couple of minutes later, in the direction of the invalid lying on the cold tarmac.

"WHAT ARE YOU DOING STEVE?"

"I'M SAVING YOUR LIFE, THANK YOU VERY MUCH!"

"BUT WHY ARE…?"

"JUST BE CAREFUL, THIS TRAFFIC COULD FLATTEN YOU BACK THERE."

"IT'S NOT GOING TO…"

"YES IT WILL IF YOU'RE NOT CAREFUL!"

"BUT STEVE…"

"I'LL COVER YOU FOR ANOTHER FEW MINUTES!"

"STEVE. I'M NOT ON THE ROAD ANY MORE."

I turned around to find Spence standing beside his upturned bike at the roadside, calmly checking the alignment of his wheels.

"WELL THANKS FOR LETTING ME KNOW, YOU DAFT GOAT."

His right pannier bag had cushioned the blow and miraculously preserved his bike in perfect working order. Treacherous metal train tracks on the road's surface were the culprit on this occasion, but thankfully no harm had been caused to Spence or his noble steed during their unceremonious tumble.

Taking our speed down a notch or two, we cautiously pedalled the remaining few miles to the quaint riverside village of Saint-Michel-de-Maurienne in the foothills of the Alps. Majestic mountains capped with snow peeked through thick, grey clouds whichever way we looked. This village felt like a gateway to the real thing. All of that could wait until morning though. We pulled up at our apartment, where we were welcomed by an eccentric retired couple who didn't speak a word of English. A creaking lift took us to the seventh floor, and they ushered us into a fusty, cluttered apartment. A typical granny flat. Spence and I stood in their narrow hallway, shivering and soaked to the bone, looking at one another. Our hosts smiled at us. We smiled back.

After resorting to charades one more time and simulating showering myself, the lady of the house – called Suzanne – finally twigged and threw me a towel. Ten minutes later, I was back in her kitchen drinking a mug of piping hot chocolate milk while Spence hopped into the bathroom. An engineering student called Robin, lodging at the house, spoke fluent English and became our translator from that point on. He'd decided not to jump in and help when we first arrived because he found our shambolic efforts at communicating with interpretative dance far more amusing.

Around the breakfast table the next day, Suzanne and Robin brought out a detailed map of the French Alps and insisted multiple times that we steer clear of Col du Galibier.

"It's not just another little hill, guys," said Robin. "It's a huge mountain."

"But we need to go over it to get to Nice from here," I replied, running my finger down the map as I spoke.

Robin finished the piece of toast he was chewing, had another sip of coffee and looked up at us. "I'm just saying, you should really try and find another way."

Cursing the entire Australian race under my breath (again), I stood out of the saddle and tried to push through the intense burning sensation that shot through my thighs with every new pedal stroke. The steepness of the roads was taking its punishing toll, and I wasn't even a quarter of the way up the day's "warm-up" mountain.

I thought back through the words I'd had spouted at me forty-five minutes earlier. "Yeah maaaaaaeeeettttt. You're gonna need a decent bike shop to look at that. There's no bloody way you're gonna get up Galibier in the big ring." He spoke with such authority. Temporarily pushing aside my inbuilt opinion of all Australians as self-obsessed prima donnas in surf shorts and sandals, I had taken this amateur cyclist at his word. He seemed different. I trusted him.

"Listen maaaaaaeeeettttt, I know exactly what you're after," he continued. "There's a humongous bike shop, yeah. I saw it this morning. Down on the main street in the town. I know it's a ball-ache cycling back down, but they'll fix you up good and proper. On the left hand side beside the post office. Go well my friend. All the best maaaaaaeeeettttt!" He clipped back into his pedals and chased to rejoin the rest of his group, his large, lycra-clad behind bouncing from side to side as he strained to turn his pedals up the incline.

It felt like a waste of so much hard work, but I knew I had to cut my losses. I'd reached the stage where my bike being stuck in the large chain ring was forcing me to stop at every second corner, gasping for air. I'd got through some tough scrapes over the previous couple of weeks, but Aussie Ausborne was right - it was impossible to go on like this.

I threw my panniers by the roadside, abandoning Spence a quarter of the way up the Col de Telegraphe (the first, much smaller mountain of the day's two planned climbs), and freewheeled back towards Saint-Michel-de-Maurienne. The descent took a painfully long time. Painful, because I was well aware that every second of effortlessly gliding down the mountain would soon equate to five seconds of gruelling climbing back up again. It had to be done though. I even felt a touch proud of my usually-stubborn self for acknowledging my need of help, and taking sensible steps to rectify the issue.

But I should have known.

Swinging around the corner on to the main street and locating the shop beside the post office, I hopped off my bike and bounded through the door. I couldn't see bikes anywhere. A few pairs of cycling shorts and a handful of polo-shirts, yes, but nothing to suggest this was a bike shop of any description, let alone a "humongous" one. The store attendant spoke a few words of English, and kindly – but confidently – told me that he knew absolutely nothing about bike maintenance. He assured me he could do a good deal on a pair of shorts, but that was the height of it. Apparently the nearest bike shop was 50km back down the road we had arrived on the previous day. Either way, I had to get to Spence to tell him. Phoning him to come down the mountain would be no good at all, having lumbered him with my three pannier bags.

The second ascent was so much harder, physically and mentally, knowing that I'd have to go down *again* once I broke the bad news to poor, long-suffering Spence. All the little fella had wanted was a light-hearted cycling holiday in the sun to get away from it all, and what he'd got in return was three days out of action with a broken bike, a heavy crash in the driving rain, and now wasn't even going to be able to boast to his work colleagues about climbing an Alpine mountain because his clueless mate didn't know how to fix a minor chain-ring issue.

It was all that thick Aussie's fault, I mumbled through the pain. Sure, I never really wanted my bike fixed anyway. A nice polo shirt is exactly what I was after. Scandalous individual. Can't believe I fell for his charm. Australians were never this annoying when me and my sister used to watch Home and Away after getting in from school.

Almost flopping into Spence's arms when I reached him again, I knew I couldn't push on any further. I keeled over under the shade of a tree and demolished a couple of cereal bars, while Spence took my bike from me. I rested my head back onto the long grass by the roadside and decided that this seemed like a good place to die. I'd gone out in style. It would be something interesting for the headstone at least – "He died valiantly attempting to cycle the length of France, and very nearly succeeded".

Fifteen seconds later, a loud shout from Spence awoke me from my daydream.

"Steve, I've got it working."

"You what?!"

"Did you even press the gear changer, you numpty?" An unbearably smug expression was etched across his face, and he didn't begin to try to cover up his joy at exposing my ineptitude.

"Yeah, like only about 15,000 times."

"Well, it's working, I'm in the small cog now. Climb on there and tell me how that feels."

I hopped back onto the all-too-familiar aluminium frame and started turning the pedals. I couldn't believe it. He'd done it. It suddenly felt so easy. Beyond easy. To think I'd not only wasted energy today in unnecessarily climbing the first part of this mountain twice, but also used up huge, huge quantities of energy that I hadn't needed to on savage climbs throughout the whole trip. All because I hadn't pressed my gear changer hard enough. Sometimes I wonder if my PE teacher at school made a fairly accurate analysis when he told me as a 13 year-old, "If brains were a disease, Stephen, you'd be healthy".

The "ease" I felt with my new-found gears lasted all of about five minutes. The gradient didn't let up, and my thighs soon started screaming again. One trademark feature of roads on mountainsides is their jagged, zig-zagging layout, forever cutting back on themselves as a means of smoothing out some of the steepness. Now firmly stuck in the granny gear, I wasn't exactly storming up but baby steps of progress were being made. Instead of stopping at every second corner like before, I could now manage about five before unclipping to catch a breather.

It was clear that Spence was coming into his own on this terrain. We have significantly different body compositions, to say the very least. Spence's spindly frame is not far off being only two thirds of my body weight. So while he effortlessly breezed ahead reminiscent of a mountain goat skipping from rock to rock, I was stuck gasping for air a few hundred metres back like an asthmatic Chihuahua who'd lost its inhaler. He was making this seem like a walk in the park.

Just at the point when my legs were contemplating seizing up and detaching themselves from the rest of my body, the road levelled out and a large wooden sign appeared welcoming us to the summit of Col de Telegraphe. A wave of relief swept over me. I turned to Spence, hugged him and got a nearby group of cyclists to take a photo of the occasion before I collapsed in a heap. Again.

Ambling into the warmth and comfort of a small coffee shop, I ordered a strong brew and three Mars bars. I ate all three before we got back on the bikes, the first one disappearing before I'd even paid for it. I shared some pictures on Facebook and Twitter using the café's free wifi, and unwisely got comfortable on a little chair perched in the corner beside a radiator. Spence was chomping at the bit to get going again. Which is a good thing, to be honest. If he hadn't been with me, I don't think I'd have ever left that café.

He physically dragged me from my seat back out into the cold air which had only got colder. We started pedalling almost immediately so I wouldn't have time to think of more excuses, and began into another one of those bittersweet downhill segments where all you can think about is your agonising work from earlier going down the pan with every metre of altitude lost. Our rapid descent eventually came to an end as we approached the town of Valloire. A ski resort during the winter months, it sits nestled at the foot of the Col de Telegraphe and marks the start line for the unrelenting 18km climb to the summit of the imposing – and quite frankly terrifying – Col du Galibier.

Refilling our water bottles in a Valloire hotel bar, and stuffing our pockets with Milka chocolate bars, we strode out to our bikes like two soldiers marching knowingly towards the scene of battle. Prior to that morning, chatting over pancakes and chocolate milk in Suzanne's kitchen, I had never heard of Galibier. We soon learnt about its fearsome reputation. With a summit of 2,645 metres, it has featured in the Tour de France over thirty times (including the brutal 2011 edition where the peloton climbed it twice on consecutive days). And in what remains my favourite Galibier fact of all, the first time it was used in the Tour back in 1911 only three cyclists made it to the top without getting off and walking.

About thirty seconds into our own climb, I could completely understand why.

I'd never climbed a mountain on a bike. I'd been on countless cycles before with sheer hills to navigate, but those had always involved fairly short bursts of effort followed by a downhill stretch to shake off the lactic. This brute looming large over the Alps did not give us a break. Just a never-ending upwards torture chamber for the thighs, with the staggeringly high peak of Galibier on the horizon more of a constant reminder of how ludicrously far we still had to go rather than a finish line to aim for.

Half way up the climb from Valloire to the Col de Galibier

The road wasn't even smooth or flat beneath us. Not even close. We had to constantly weave our front wheels from side to side to dodge potholes. There were buckets of debris to contend with too. For much of the early climb the road was speckled with not just pebbles, but decent-sized stones – some not much smaller than golf balls – and so the ground felt like it was moving underneath us with every pedal stroke we took.

Arguably the finest climber in world cycling today is Nairo Quintana, the pint-sized Colombian and winner of two Grand Tours who (when he's on form) attacks his fellow competitors on mountain climbs for fun. Known by his travelling supporters as 'Nairoman' or the *escarabajo* – flying beetle – he tips the scales at a measly 58kg. That's 9 stone. And he's got calf muscles tighter than my old jeans after Christmas dinner. My fighting weight, after a really solid block of training, sits at just over 12 stone. That's an extra three stones I'm carrying up every climb. The weight of an elephant's heart, I'm reliably informed. Now there's a challenge for the future – me vs Nairo Quintana with an elephant's heart strapped to his back, up a mountain of his choice, first to the top wins.

My muscles were stinging with pain now. When nearing my physical limits, I do this slightly unusual thing where I almost go into a trance. I start to focus really deliberately on my breathing in the hope that it'll distract me from the pain my body's going through. I find myself doing this during hard run sessions at the athletics track or in the last five minutes of a spinning class. Without realising, I was now employing this strategy as I very slowly progressed up Galibier's slopes – counting pedal strokes in a repetitive cycle to coincide with each breath I was taking, "In, 2, 3, 4, Out, 2, 3, 4".

I also began singing to the rhythm of my pedal strokes. That day, "Let it Snow" was on loop in my head, over and over again. Inspired by my surroundings I hummed and whistled and groaned along like a broken Christmas jukebox. And once I got going, I couldn't shake it off. I don't even like the song.

I was clutching at straws for anything to keep my mind detached from my body. From my own experience, employing mental distraction has allowed me to achieve far more sporting goals than physical training alone ever could have. You're obviously not going to run a marathon if you never do any run training, but the fittest person in the world won't finish a marathon if they don't have a strategy in place to block out the wall of pain when it inevitably comes along.

"This is the hardest thing I've ever done," I gasped in Spence's direction. "No question."

He grunted his approval as he flicked down a gear or two and fought to turn the pedals. "How are the legs holding up, Steve?"

"They're not. I'm dying back here."

As we pulled over for a quick drink, I hoked around in my bag for more clothes. The mad effect of altitude on the temperature was hitting home. For the past hour or so I had been wearing nothing on my top half except an unzipped-to-the-bellybutton lycra cycling jersey. However the higher we advanced up the spiky, back and forth ascent, the more it felt like we were pedalling into a gigantic freezer. By the time we were 10km from the summit I had four layers of clothing on, with a massive coat thrown on top. And still my teeth hammered together everytime I stopped to catch my breath. I remember thinking, this had better be a really, really good view. Or else.

The further my weary legs pushed me upwards, the more I displayed very clear signs of the effects the thin air was having on me. I was going more than a little bit high. I've never taken recreational drugs, but I don't imagine they'd cause me to spew more nonsense than what I did towards the top of that climb. Missing out words, suddenly finding unfunny things very, very funny and chatting like a four year-old child who'd just discovered ice cream for the first time.

I later found a video saved on my phone (which I can't remember taking), recorded eight kilometres from the summit.

"Have a loooook at this! Wow! That is…aaaahhh. Tell you what…that is an amazing…yeah. That is a mountain. And THIS is a mountain too! It's huge. This mountain is called…I can't remember. But LOOK AT IT! I love that. It's very cold."

I wasn't finished there.

"But I've got gloves. My yellow gloves! I put them on today to keep my hands warm. Well, I've actually just taken them off to make this video. But I should probably put them back on. Because it's so cold! I love my gloves."

Imagine if my body had been found weeks later after collapsing from fatigue and hypothermia, and all that was left as a record of how I went was that video and a child-like smile etched on my face, having passed away thinking only of how much I loved my yellow gloves.

Creeping up the final, steepest third so slowly it felt like I was going in reverse, the distance markers quickly became all that occupied my thoughts. Each new kilometre that passed, tiny stone structures on either side of the road indicated how many still remained and what the average gradient would be for the coming kilometre. In its entirety, Galibier runs at an average gradient of 7%, and spikes up to as much as 10% for the final, cruel slog to the peak. One more marker, I kept telling myself.

Snow stood over head height on either side of the road with three kilometres to go. The cold up this high was a bitter cold. I told Spence to ride on to the summit ahead of me, while I alternated between walking and cycling, a minute at a time. During one short spell on the bike, I shuffled past a deflated Dutch cyclist hunched over his bike by the roadside. I stopped to check if he was still alive, and promised to look out for him at the top if we ever made it there.

Three corners later, at a steeper gradient than anywhere else on the mountain, a wooden hut appeared. Spence stood beside it. The entrance to a dark tunnel sat on the other side of the road, which my Dutch friend had told me was the final stretch to the summit. We were standing in the clouds now, and it wasn't getting any less icy. Side by side, we turned on our bike lights and edged through the tunnel towards the light.

And then, oh my days.

I almost crashed into a lamppost, so fixed were my eyes on the most breathtaking sight they've ever stumbled upon. It didn't seem right that we could go from murky, suffocating skies on one side of a tunnel and arrive at this on the other. More mountain peaks than anyone could possibly count opened up in front of us, with ribbon roads weaving between them into the valley below.

King of all I survey at the top of Galibier, feeling more than a little knocked off

Frozen and off my rocker, I started taking off layers and stormed around shouting "Give me my Northern Ireland top!" This was borderline dangerous. It's well known that one of the last things people suffering from extreme hypothermia do before dying is remove all their clothes, in the false assumption that they're burning up with heat. Not that I had a baldy about what I was up to.

Spence stood in the doorway of the coffee shop at the summit, yelling "Come on in, Steve, it's Baltic out there!"

We quickly photographed the occasion and hopped inside, where the shop-owner welcomed us by exclaiming that a group of cyclists from Coleraine had passed by an hour before us. Turns out he wasn't messing around either, and they were friends of Spence's. Of all the places to just miss meeting a bunch of old mates from home. Another sign that every corner of France was slowly being taken over by the Green and White Army.

With hands gradually defrosting as we cradled mugs of hot chocolate in the café, we looked out the window at the quite frankly bonkers panoramic view. Our shop-owner friend pulled up a wooden bench alongside us, and explained that the rapid 35km descent to our accommodation in Briançon wouldn't even take an hour. I didn't care. I wasn't going anywhere near a bike again in a hurry.

The glide down from the summit – when we mustered the energy to leave our mountain top café – was an hour of otherworldly beauty. I have never witnessed scenery like it in my life. I was torn between pedalling harder to ramp up the wide-eyed excitement of speeding downhill out of each turn, and applying the brakes to somehow prolong the dazzling display of nature around me.

Briançon, in the valley below Galibier, had its own selection of spectacular views but – after a long day cycling – it wasn't exactly swimming with decent places to grab a bite. Going for dinner that night in a popular American fast food chain that will remain unnamed, we returned to its irresistible golden arches early the following morning for an additional calorie top-up.

As I chewed into my lukewarm Chicken Legend, I flicked through a copy of Le Dauphiné that had been left on a table. Euro 2016 had hit the front pages. After months of hype, the football was ready for lift-off with the opening game between hosts France and Romania that evening in Paris (over four hundred and fifty miles away).

We delayed our departure while I waited to go on air for an interview on live radio, much to Spence's dismay. I could see the effect it was having on him and his increasingly itchy feet. Every extra minute I sat with my feet up waiting to go on air with the phone to my ear, Spence would pace up and down mumbling in a panicked tone, "We have to go Steve. We'll never make it. You've done more than enough radio, just tell them you're too busy. Sure, does anyone actually listen to it anyway?"

Having wrapped up my 45-second interview slot, I chased Spence as he shot off like a rocket to make amends for the time we'd lost. We didn't speak for the next half an hour, partly because my lax approach to timekeeping was frustrating the life out of him, and partly because he was so occupied with recovering a healthy number of miles in the three remaining hours before lunch. I just about clung on to his tail.

Caked in sun tan lotion, our two-man peloton raced out of town along the Durance river in the direction of Embrun. I don't think I've ever seen colours as vivid. Clumps of bright pink flowers sat scattered through fields in sharp contrast to the paper-white, snow-capped peaks and pristine blue sky. We even took the chance to have a quick splash at a small roadside lake, with sunbathing parents frantically reaching to protect their children's eyes from the sight of two lunatics leaping into the water wearing nothing but indecently skimpy bib shorts.

The terrain was either flat or slightly downhill all the way to Embrun, sitting at the eastern end of the Lac de Serre-Poncon. Which, despite its name, isn't a lake. Instead it's a monumentally large reservoir. And one that we spent most of the rest of the day trying to circumnavigate. Our ascent from the day before unfortunately hadn't spelt the end to our uphill struggles. There were more than a few soul-shattering climbs to negotiate as we lumbered over mountain passes around the perimeter of the lake.

The solitary road that headed in the direction of Nice was immediately across the lake from where we started, and sadly it was far too vast a body of water for a bridge ever to be built. To be fair, we had made it significantly harder by taking on board the most disgracefully large lunch at a roadside restaurant in Savines-le-Lac before tackling the treacherous high roads. Combined with our jelly-legged hangover from Galibier, it wasn't cycling at its most elegant.

With light falling from the sky that evening, we gratefully rolled into Digne-les-Bains. Our last overnight stop-off before the welcoming arms of Nice. We locked our bikes in a damp, dusty cupboard under the stairs at our hostel and looked for somewhere to watch the France game, that had just kicked off as far as we were aware. Not that you could tell from the scenes on the empty streets of Digne. Eerie silence all around. But let's not be hard on our French friends, we thought. Maybe they're all inside bars and restaurants watching on big screens.

Nope. Not a soul. Digne clearly isn't the footballing hotbed of France. We couldn't find a single joint in the whole of the town showing the action. After one further unsuccessful circuit of the town's cobbled streets, we grabbed a couple of hot dogs from a chippy van and retreated to our hostel to watch the second half on the miniature TV in our bedroom, cobwebs dangling from its oversized aerial.

The clunking noises of market stalls being assembled underneath our window in the morning had us awake well before dawn. I would have struggled to sleep anyway. The big day had arrived. Blue road signs had already started pointing the way to Nice. We wolfed down a breakfast of sugared pastries at our hostel with two young German couples before heading on our way. I attempted to intimidate them with fighting talk ahead of our upcoming match, bragging about how Steve Davis was the player Thomas Müller dreamt of becoming. They didn't find this funny. At all. Safe to say, sarcasm isn't the national language of Germany.

This was a day of celebration though. I'd received a video call early that morning from my brother, who'd safely set up camp with Mum and Dad on the outskirts of Nice, and had spent the past couple of days revelling amidst yachts and supercars in Monaco and Cannes. Alright for some. We agreed to meet them for lunch, and three hours later the grand reunion took place at a creperie in Castellane. Pears and chocolate sauce on top of hot pancakes, with a naughty scoop of ice-cream thrown on the side for good measure. Downright sensational.

Despite now having the family for moral support and regular croissant pit-stops, there were still lumps and bumps in the landscape to clamber over, but the sea was – for the first time – becoming detectable through the summery haze on the horizon.

On one particularly steep road, Spence and I overtook the same elderly cyclist for the third time that day. Each time we stopped for a food break or a puncture repair, he'd go ahead of us again. But we'd always work our way back to him. We had noticed that he was grinding out an excruciatingly high gear, and pulled alongside him as he grunted along at snail pace.

"Bonjour!" I shouted "Comment t'appeles tu?"

"Moi? Je m'appelle Jean" he gasped back.

"Tu parles anglais?"

"Ehhh yes, but just a little".

He must have been at least seventy, and couldn't have looked more stereotypically French in his cloth cycling cap and yellow jersey unzipped to reveal the wispy grey hair on his well-weathered, sun-bronzed chest.

"Do you have a small cog?" asked Spence, signalling towards Jean's back wheel.

"Yes, of course"

"You should use it on these hills. It is much, much easier."

Jean looked at Spence, then at me, sweat dripping from his brow on to the ground below as he turned his head. He looked slightly offended by our advice. The exhausted grimace on his face slowly turned into a smile as he lifted his head once more and pointedly gave us his reply.

"For big Jean, *always* the big cog."

Over the crest of yet another 'Col' on the undulating route down to Nice

We patted him on the back, handed him a banana for the road, and wished him well. For the next fifty miles or so, we sporadically played 'Big Jean's Challenge', where we would crunch up nasty climbs in the highest gear, yelling at one another "*Always* the big cog!" The miles Jean must have racked up over his lifetime would be frightening. I tried to bottle some of his passion and enthusiasm as we continued on towards the coast.

Stretching out to the horizon in front of me, the deep blue of the Mediterannean Sea shimmered in the sunlight and left me speechless.

I could feel a very real lump in my throat. The last time I saw open water was two weeks before as I stumbled off the ferry in the fog at Cherbourg. Feeling like Moses looking out over the promised land after forty years wandering in the wilderness, I stood there stunned. All the anguished hill climbs and hideous headwinds of the past fortnight took on fresh significance. I might sound like a nutcase for saying it, but I was thankful for every ache, pain and obstacle I'd had to overcome, because of what I'd arrived at. It felt like a far greater and more satisfying reward because I'd had to earn it.

So many things flooded my mind. I'd literally climbed mountains to be here.

The view I'd been dreaming of for weeks - The crystal blue of the Côte d'Azur

Tens of thousands of football fans from all walks of life in Northern Ireland had now travelled over as well, and by staying absolutely silent for a few moments you could almost convince yourself you could hear them singing. Which you obviously couldn't, with us still being twenty miles from Nice and all that. But in my head they were singing.

Dipping sharply towards sea level, we left the sparse hills behind and began to freewheel past tanned joggers, suited businessmen and spritely dog walkers. In other words, we were returning to civilisation. Signs started appearing for our campsite, and it was like we had gained a set of completely fresh legs. We felt like marathon runners who had hit the proverbial wall, got back up and from some inexplicable reserve found a sprint finish.

Narrow roads weaved left, then right, then left again. Hedgerows and holiday apartments fizzed past so quickly they were a barely distinguishable blur in the corners of our eyes. I couldn't think of a time when I'd felt this alive on a bike before. The sandy-coloured brick wall of the campsite's entrance appeared so suddenly on the left side of the road that we careered past it before even noticing where we were.

A swift U-turn put that right, and Spence and I rolled back through the gate into Les Pinèdes campsite. And in a ludicrous turn of events that would almost make you think the original architect of the site had heard we were coming and wanted one last laugh at our expense, there was an unreasonably sharp hill in front of us before reaching the main camping area.

I took a Northern Ireland shirt out of my pannier bag and handed it to Spence. This was an important moment for him to share in. I'd been wearing my kaleidoscopic 1992 retro home shirt all day over my bib shorts, but I felt like a proud dad with his son as I watched Spence – with his blatant disregard for football – pulling on the green and white. Standing up out of our saddles, we drove our ailing legs one last time up the hill.

And then something incredible happened.

My family had arrived at the campsite three days before us, and mentioned in passing to a couple of other Northern Ireland fans about our imminent arrival. Once word leaked out, the GAWA members on the campsite expressed a desire to make it a welcome to remember. Most probably because they'd run out of Buckfast and were looking for something to do with their spare time until the football kicked off. Still, it didn't make it any less special.

Pushing upwards, I spotted my brother, Andrew, standing at the top of the hill with his camera-phone aloft, recording our arrival. I couldn't help but laugh. It was hard to believe this was happening. A few more turns of the pedals, and my journey the length of France would be complete. A faint ripple of applause filtered through the air, and grew in volume as more and more people joined in. Loud cheers and whistles started to ring out too, but I couldn't see who or where they were coming from.

Out of nowhere, a man I'd never met ran into my line of vision and stood beside Andrew, his face alive with energy, shouting "Go on my son!" Turning the corner and cycling past him, I realised he wasn't alone.

An unforgettable guard of honour stood spread out in front of Spence and I. Dozens of Northern Ireland fanatics lined each side of the path, with NI flags draped on clothes-lines over an impromptu finishing tunnel. The noise reached fever pitch as we savoured the last few metres, people running beside us and patting us on the backs while we pedalled past. I finally clipped out and planted my feet on solid ground.

Instantly, I was swept up in a sea of football-loving Northern Ireland natives wanting to shake my hand. And not just any old handshakes, but the sort of honest, heartfelt, risk-leaving-you-with-a-couple-of-fractured-fingers sort of handshakes that you'll only ever get from an impassioned Ulsterman.

The glorious homecoming in Nice

The small but raucous crowd had invited a group of German supporters from a nearby tent to join in with the celebrations. Three people in Northern Ireland shirts offered me a drink there and then, while another fan promised me one the next time he saw me due to the fact that he'd finished his own personal supply earlier that afternoon. One man shouted in the direction of his slightly rotund mate, "Can we get you a pair of those lycra shorts, John? The ladies in Nice wouldn't know what had hit them!" Another grabbed me firmly by the shoulder and pulled me in for a hug.

Just *look* at all these people, I thought to myself. These are exactly the kind of people that make me love Northern Ireland and what it represents so much. Glancing at the worryingly red colour of their skin after only a couple of days on the south coast of France, you could tell that many of them weren't used to holidays like this. Or at least weren't used to using sun cream. A bare-chested, tattooed man with an east Belfast accent as broad as his shoulders waded alongside me, thumped me square in the back and said "Congratulations big lawd. Outstanding work." In any other setting you'd be concerned that a man of his build might fancy taking you out the back for a fight. Turns out he just wanted a selfie.

Half an hour later, the crowd dispersed back to their caravans, and Spence and I trudged the final few steps to the mobile home my family had rented on the site. Mum had overloaded plates of bolognese lined up when we threw the bikes aside and collapsed into the arms of two of the campsite's plastic patio chairs. As we tucked into dinner, the inhabitants of the caravan next door launched into their fifth rendition in a row of the George Best 'Spirit in the Sky' song.

"They haven't stopped for the past two days, day or night," said Dad chuckling and shaking his head with disbelief.

We stayed up late into the night sharing tales from life on the road, with "Sweet Caroline" ringing in our ears. I couldn't think of any people I'd rather have spent that night with than my family. Some of the only people who genuinely believed I could make it this far, and now we were all kicking back together with the Mediterranean in sight. I poured myself another drink as the sun began to set behind the pine trees.

"It's crazy. The plane the other day took two hours to fly over France," said Andrew. "We were looking out the window, thinking how mad it was you were doing that on a bike."

"I know, it's a brilliant achievement," chimed Mum. "You should both make sure you enjoy a decent night's rest now you've finished."

In one sense my mum was absolutely right – we had finished. I'd cycled France top to bottom. But with the first NI match at a major championship in three decades now less than twenty-four hours away, the real fun was only just getting started.

Two very happy campers at Les Pinèdes caravan site, Nice

"I've been running a poorly paid taxi service since the day we arrived here," joked Dad, as he flicked on the indicators and waited for his next passenger to climb aboard.

"Did none of them rent cars?" I said, eating a dry baguette and winding up my window to see if the air con might cool things down a notch.

"I don't think any of them realised just how far they were from the city."

The old man and his super sleek hire car had become the talking point of our campsite.

Punters were slowly learning of the twenty kilometres that separated our accommodation from the middle of Nice. The camp's website had chosen to avoid including that little snippet of information. And considering that five minutes in the glare of the midday sun was enough to force most travelling Northern Irish supporters to remove t-shirts and place them over their sunburnt balding heads for shelter, it was unlikely that any of them would have survived the four-hour hike to the fanzone.

I rolled the window down once more, and shouted "Green and White Army!" at the middle-aged man ambling along the pavement behind us. We'd had a monumental amount of fun playing this game all morning. Rules are simple – you lean out the car window and blurt the four magic words in the face of any passer-by dressed in green, and if they respond in kind they earn themselves a lift into town. The responses we got, especially from groups of ten people or more, were a magical sound to be met with as we cruised along in the sunshine.

Ninety-nine percent of people responded with the most over-the-top, heart-on-their-sleeve cries anyone could possibly hope for, but our latest man just smiled and waved back at us. I was instantly suspicious. How can he not know the rules of the shouting game? I didn't feel comfortable with him from the word go.

"Hi there, where are you heading?" Dad shouted out the window, as the mysterious character skipped towards us and hopped into the back seat beside Mum and Andrew.

"Just down to the train station, boss," he said in his broad American twang. "I'm Paddy. Really appreciate this. That heat's wild out there!"

"You don't have any spare tickets, Paddy?" I called into the back as we moved off. "Just Andrew here doesn't have one, and he'd love to get a bit of the big match atmosphere."

Paddy sniffed an opportunity for some sly holiday profiteering. You could hear the leather squeak beneath him as he shuffled to the edge of his seat.

"Funny you should ask," he quipped without hesitation. "I've got an extra ticket from a mate who sadly can't make it, and I could do you a very good deal on it."

"What are we talking?"

"Well, it cost him 120 euros, but I could maybe do a special mate's rate of 100 euros. Let me just phone to check with him first. He's down at the fanzone."

I quietly reached into my pocket, and unfolded the 25 euro ticket that I'd carried every inch of the journey around France with me. Either Paddy's spare ticket was for a seat that was literally hovering above the centre circle, or he was being a cowboy. I knew for a fact no tickets for this game were being sold at that price. And anyway, what on earth was his "mate" doing in Nice if he couldn't make the game?

Paddy's accent belied the Northern Ireland replica shirt on his back for starters. He claimed to have moved to the province when he was young, but he wasn't convincing me. I mulled things over while he pretended to chat on the phone. If this "mate" couldn't make it due to illness, then surely any price would be a bonus. Otherwise he's just losing a ticket with nothing in return.

He came off the phone, and I made an offer.

"We could give you fifty euros, Paddy, but no more than that." He probably wasn't even called Paddy. That was clearly just the most stereotypically Irish name that popped into his devious, money-hungry little brain.

"Aaaaah, afraid I can't do that. My friend would be losing a huge amount then."

The train station mercifully appeared soon after, and we ushered Paddy on his way. I watched him closely as he walked away, and before long he was troubling another unsuspecting group of Northern Ireland fans with his extortionate dealings. I wonder where he'd swindled the shirt from. The boy wouldn't know he was in Belfast if the City Hall was staring him in the face.

That chancer aside, the streets were paved top to bottom with giddily excited supporters. This was the day we'd been impatiently waiting on for what seemed like forever. Even in the suburbs, grown adults wearing comedy green wigs and berets could be found letting rip with the sort of uninhibited singing you'd normally only see after two or three hours of substantial alcoholic encouragement at a karaoke night. It was just like we were making our way down Donegall Avenue towards Windsor Park on a match night, only with slightly more sunshine in the sky and slightly less Union Jack bunting hanging from the lampposts.

Spence unfortunately was missing out.

Shortly after seven o'clock that morning the gang of us had crept stealthily past our snoring, hungover fellow campers and travelled to Nice Airport before anyone on the south coast had even entertained the thought of waking up. At least that's the way it felt as we breezed along yawning, empty roads.

When he'd booked flights originally, Spence had made it clear he didn't care when the football was taking place, as long as he got a good whack of cycling in. But as he methodically placed parts of his bike into a large cardboard box in a secluded corner of the airport terminal, still wearing the Northern Ireland shirt I'd lent him from the night before, you could see it in his eyes. He even admitted that part of him wished he could stick around and enjoy the big occasion with the ever-growing throng of expectant supporters emerging through arrival gates around us.

"So you promise me you'll find somewhere to watch it later?" I said as he threw his backpack over his shoulder.

"You never know. At least I know a few of the songs now."

"Good lad. I'll catch you back in the homeland."

He turned and made his way to passport control. A hefty line of people were queued in front of him, and so me and mum stood against the back wall and waited to wave him off. Ten minutes later when he'd almost reached the desk, I shouted one last time in his direction.

"Hey Spence…"

He turned his head and looked back at us.

"…GREEN AND WHITE ARMY!"

He didn't open his mouth in response, but soon cracked a smile as a crowd of boisterous Northern Ireland fans echoed my cry over to the right of where we were standing. We watched Spence meander through check-in, and just like that I was a lone cyclist again. From here until Paris it was going to be me, myself and I powering along the ribbon roads. But issues like that could wait until tomorrow.

"I'm gonna die out here!" howled Andrew, using his sleeve to wipe another stream of sweat from his cheek.

It was like a heat switch had been flicked on overnight. After stepping off the bus that was ferrying football fans from the city centre towards the Stade de Nice, a seemingly endless pilgrimage lay before us with the stadium a faint, hazy blob on the horizon.

Andrew hadn't been able to get a ticket, but joined me for the Saharan trek to the gates to soak up the buzz anyway. The Allianz Riviera, to give the ground its corporate title, is perched six miles west of Nice's city centre on the banks of the Var river. And the stifling hike there would have been a good sight more bearable if water from the river had been left in buckets for us to chuck over one another.

"You think that big boy's ever been let out in the sun before?" I asked, nodding towards a topless, mildly inebriated individual up ahead. There was plenty of him to go around too, his beetroot-red belly hanging far below his waistline.

"Oh wow," laughed Andrew. "That is a painful skin colour."

"There's no way he's gonna last two hours in this," I said, shaking my head in disbelief. Wearing a miniscule sun hat to keep his shaven head cool but leaving his hippopotamus-sized shoulders and back at the mercy of the French Riviera's weather gods, I didn't know whether to question his choice of clothing or his mental wellbeing.

We mingled with Polish fans outside the ground, who it must be said look considerably more approachable when lathered in face paint. I remember going on tour with my university football team a few years back, where we found ourselves repeatedly kicked out of nightclubs in Wroclaw by terrifying skinheaded Polish bouncers. And since then, that has been the abiding image in my mind of what all Poles must be like. Turns out a bit of red and white on their cheeks is all that is needed to remove the fear factor.

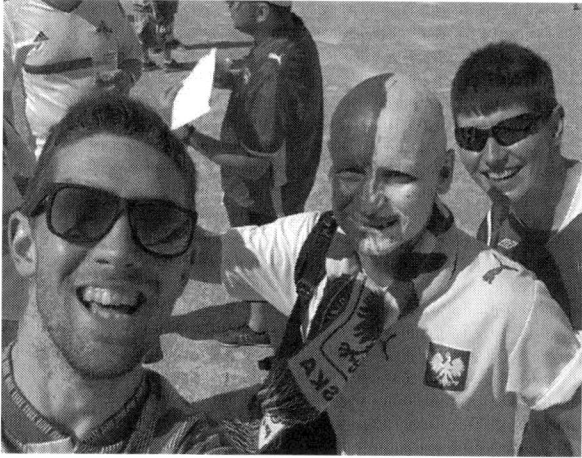

Bit of face paint slapped on their cheeks, and they're a barrel of laughs

Once I'd parted ways with Andrew, I removed my sunglasses and gasped at the futuristic marvel of a stadium in front of me with coloured shirts buzzing in and out of it. The undulating architecture took my breath away, with shards of silver jutting out in dramatic contours above my head.

"Here, you!" came a brash voice from nearby.

A middle-aged couple in Northern Ireland tops shuffled towards me. I didn't recognise either of them.

"Aren't you that cycling guy?" asked the man.

"Yeah, I suppose so. Have we met before?"

"No, mate," he replied. "Just saw your write-up in the Belfast Telegraph the arrrrr day."

(For those who don't have friends from Northern Ireland, mirror = mrrrrr, power = parrrrr, shower = sharrrrr, and other = arrrrrr)

"G'wan, let's have a wee look at your cyalves then," added his wife unashamedly, in her treacle-thick Derry accent.

Derry/Londonderry/The Walled City/The Maiden City/Stroke City is a contentiously-named spot close to Northern Ireland's border with County Donegal, where people called Cyarol drive in their cyars to buy cyat food at the supermarket.

"Don't remember your cyalves ever looking as tight as them things, Harry!" she barked at her long-suffering husband.

I posed for a quick photo and scurried towards the entrance to the Northern Ireland fans' section of the ground before I needed to place a restraining order on Harry's wife.

The steps inside the stand went on and on and on. After several flights of stairs, blinking in the shimmering sunlight as I climbed, a disorderly crowd of green and white busied about in front of me. Samba drums rang through the air – thanks to two tournament-sponsored musicians dropped in the middle of our fans to get the party started, not because our resident drummers had learnt some adventurous new rhythms – and grown Northern Irish men belied their age and their arthritis as each one took it in turn to show off their most exotic Latino dance moves.

Not only had we brought our entire fanbase to the south of France, but others on the fringes had joined in too. I bumped into friends who I'd never see at standard Windsor Park home games. It was a joy to behold. I've never understood people who criticise others for jumping on to the bandwagon when it comes to supporting our football team. I wanted to hear the green and white bandwagon creak under the weight of new fans coming on board. The larger the crowd, the bigger the army.

Vocal support was never going to be an issue for us, but still I was stunned when I strode past the transparent walls at the top of the stairwell and turned towards the pitch. A sense of feverish anticipation, mixed with vertigo, swept over me as I staggered into position amongst the deafening chorus of supporters in the top tier.

Taking my place between an elderly gent from Ballymena and a dark-haired lady called Debbie from Dungannon, it wasn't long before the teams emerged from the tunnel. The chants rang out incessantly, creating a monumental wall of noise. Both sides lined up for the anthems, like an indistinguishable row of coloured ants so far were they beneath us. As the final note was sung, the bass drum kicked into life. All those years saving up pocket money to sneak through the turnstiles and sing from the stands at Windsor were only practice for this moment. The rehearsals were over, and it was showtime.

It didn't take long for the weight of the task at hand to hit home though.

To say we were hanging on slightly in the first half would be like saying Lance Armstrong was slightly creative when it came to looking for marginal gains and North Korea are slightly disapproving of stag parties arriving dressed as Kim Jong Un. The Poles exposed us repeatedly with their pace and trickery, especially down the flanks.

Poor Conor McLaughlin, a sensational full back with a long international career ahead of him, struggled in particular and didn't feature again in the tournament. Even Michael O'Neill admitted post-match – with more than a hint of understatement – that we were "at times overpowered" in the opening forty-five minutes.

On returning from a pit stop at half-time, I tripped over the concrete steps leading back to my seat, and sliced my right shin wide open. With a pool of my blood rapidly gathering at my feet, Debbie came to my rescue by pouring bottled water over my leg and thrusting a travel pack of Kleenex into my hands. To be fair, it was the most drama we'd seen since kick off.

More bite was on display from our boys in the second half, but we couldn't hold the tide back forever. The prodigious Arkadiusz Milik – who moved from Ajax to Napoli for 35 million Euros immediately after the tournament – drove the ball through the legs of Craig Cathcart and low to our goalkeeper's left with fifty minutes on the clock. The closest we got to pegging back the deficit was an outrageous overhead effort from Kyle Lafferty that troubled his tailbone on landing significantly more than it troubled the Polish goal frame.

It just wasn't to be our day. Kyle described in the press conference afterwards how the team had felt "overawed". It was noticeable from the stands. But it was a learning curve, on and off the pitch. Those of us who had travelled to support them weren't used to this kind of occasion either. We weren't sure how long our French footballing journey would last, and so we were determined to make the most of it. The 10,000 fans packed into our end of the ground did not leave, or stop singing, for forty-five minutes after the final whistle. We hadn't won. And that felt OK. I'm not saying I was accepting defeat gladly, but just being at the top table and getting our players' unsung faces plastered on TV screens across Europe felt massive. The dream had *finally* become a reality. That was enough for today.

Four days later, we knew that Ukraine would represent a much more surmountable obstacle. And let's not forget, Poland – despite our lack of attacking verve – were very nearly nullified, with the only space enjoyed by Lewandowski being the space inside Jonny Evans' back pocket. We might not have a natural goal-getter of that calibre and we are never going to win by a handful of goals, but our defence stubbornly ensure that we're unlikely to lose by many either. Cagey is how we do things. Big tackles, long throws and set pieces. It's the only way teams of our stature are capable of competing at this level and every once in a while, it works. Just ask Iceland.

We wandered into the early evening haze with Polish versions of our own chants contributing to the melting pot of noise on the long amble back to the bus stop. Little did we know at that moment in time that, the following morning, one young Northern Irish fan called Darren would tragically lose his life falling from a beachside promenade. Or that a month later this beautiful city would be subject to a devastating terrorist attack on the Promenade des Anglais claiming the lives of eighty-six people.

Such awful events provided an acute sense of perspective, prompting universal sympathy for the families affected, and encouraging us to be more thankful for the things we are able to enjoy. For this and a whole host of other things besides, Nice remained a place etched in our minds long after the summer had passed us by.

After my first day in over two weeks without any cycling, I expected it to feel like medieval torture climbing back aboard my saddle. That grating pain that reared its head every morning, and stuck around until I shuffled into the one position that enabled me to just about tolerate it for the remainder of the day. Although still noticeable as I pulled out of the campsite in Nice and moved towards the seafront, it wasn't nearly as bad as I'd feared.

In fact, I'd missed it.

Not the burning pain between my legs, but cycling. I'd missed the prickly heat warming my skin, wind blowing the cobwebs of tiredness off (I am the world's worst morning person) and the therapeutic mind-massage of careering along narrow, unfamiliar roads towards towns that you've never even heard of before, let alone seen.

With the glistening Mediterranean Sea appearing over the ridge in front of me, I found a side-road to answer a call from Radio Ulster with reflections on the day before. Brimming with enthusiasm as questions were fired from everyone's favourite larger than life radio host, Stephen Nolan, I described the ear-splitting pre-match atmosphere, the wonderfully warm interactions with our Polish counterparts, and our team's resilient efforts in so nearly accomplishing our gameplan of squeaking out a draw against such a potent strikeforce.

We'd reached the promised land of a major tournament, the sun had got its hat on, and every Northern Ireland fan in France seemed fully intent on enjoying the ride, whether in defeat or victory. Supporters in green and white waved and cheered over at me from the other side of the road as they shuffled out of their accommodation to source some breakfast. If you hadn't been watching the match, you honestly wouldn't have been able to tell that we'd lost a game of football.

On the other end of the phone line, however, all I heard was drudgery, criticism and moaning. I really don't know where they find the unique characters for phone-ins on radio programmes in Northern Ireland. People who spend their lives whining about the abject state of our country compared to the rest of the world, and about how nobody cares for the needs of their "community". As if they're all some kind of Mandela figures speaking on behalf of their housing estate.

The other two callers on at the same time as me were the gloomiest Northern Ireland "fan" in existence who'd watched on telly and concluded that we were far too negative and didn't deserve to play at this level, and an old crank with no interest in football who dwelt solely on the fan violence before England's opener in Marseille the day before our match.

I accepted the challenge of trying to breathe a gust of positivity into the debate. I didn't intend to become the French ambassador for Northern Ireland that morning, but no-one else was stepping forward. Describing the exemplary people I'd encountered, I think I cut through some of the doom and gloom thrown out by the armchair critics. Life's too short to let people like miserable Martin in Magherafelt tell you what to think.

I was well aware that this was going to be the longest day of my entire trip. 130 miles from Nice to Aix-en-Provence, to start making tracks up towards Lyon. The only problem was that on the map it didn't look like that was taking me up at all, but instead down.

With Nice tucked in the most awkward spot imaginable for a French cycling tour, in a pokey corner next to the Italian border, I knew I'd have to shuffle west at some point. And with the Alps towering just above where Nice lay on the map, there is honestly no money on this good earth of ours that would have convinced me to head back through there for a laugh. If flat roads meant adding some mileage, then so be it.

A handful of miles later, and the red carpet was all that was missing. Talk about taking a look at how the other half live.

Nice hadn't exactly been shabby, but Cannes was mesmerising. Luxury hotels and restaurants sprung up from every patch of land, and row upon row of superyachts gleamed brightly in the iridescent water to my left. Outrageously attractive people sauntered up and down the wide boulevards. It was such a stark contrast to anything I'd seen over the previous fortnight. Host to the international Cannes Film Festival each May, it's essentially a massive bay on the Cote d'Azur swamped with rich, famous, good-looking people. And my guess is that if you don't meet all three of those criteria, you're likely to be outlawed from setting foot in the place.

My plan was to hug the shoreline until I reached Fréjus, a beautiful Ancient Roman seaside resort twenty-five miles further along the coastal road. It's also the home of Belinda Carlisle, apparently. Humming '*Heaven is a Place on Earth*' as I dodged immaculately-sculpted beachgoers, I became aware that I was losing sight of the sea. Despite my best efforts, the road system kept pulling me inland, as if to encourage my sort to get out as quickly as possible before my pasty skin and ungroomed facial hair dragged the reputation of the place down.

I got lost for over an hour. The complex network of roads would not allow me to leave, and my predicament only dawned on me when I climbed the same hill for the third time. Clearly nobody in Cannes has ever used a bicycle before. To be fair, would you bother if you had a different Lamborghini for each day of the week?

After rediscovering the deep blue, I pushed on through Fréjus and swept upwards along roads cutting through the sun-soaked red rocks of the coastline. At the bottom of one descent, a sandy beach sprung into view on my left. I couldn't cycle the length of France and *not* get my feet wet in the Mediterranean.

Chaining my bike to a rusty road sign, I clambered down the stone steps in my cleats and claimed a patch of sand. The beach was roughly a hundred metres long, and ten or twelve other people were lying prostrate soaking up the rays. I'd never seen sea look so inviting. Having grown up taking December dips in the icy waters of Portrush and Downhill, I fought hard to restrain myself. I looked around. Gorgeous, bronze-skinned people sunbathed either side of me, their skin colour blending into the sand they lay on. Ten minutes passed. Still nobody moved a muscle. I was being burnt like a crisp, and decided I could take it no more.

Stomping clumsily and impatiently into the gently rippling waves, I was fully submerged in less than ten seconds. I held my breath under the surface and basked beneath the cool water before emerging and shaking my hair out of my eyes. With the ferocious heat hitting me once more, I flapped both arms to throw as much water as I was able over my sun-scorched head. I glanced back to the shore, and the same gorgeous, bronze-skinned people were now all peering over their aviator sunglasses in my direction. Quietly wondering who this imposter was with the audacity to intrude on their secluded corner of paradise, as I splashed about in my bib shorts like a demented hippo in mating season.

"What am I getting you then?" shouted Mum.

"Crunchie McFlurry, please" I replied. "Nah, make that two."

As the long days of cycling became more physically draining, my interest in sampling traditional French cuisine had started to wane. The Collins support car had one more day in France before flying homewards the following morning. And with temperatures sitting in the high thirties for the vast majority of the afternoon, I needed their back-up.

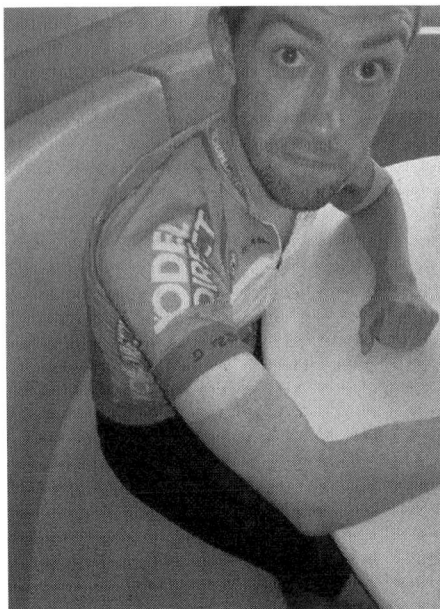

My arm starting to resemble a Neapolitan ice-cream

"Have you any more water in the car there?" I asked.

"Nope, we're down to half a bottle of warm orange juice," said Andrew.

"That'll do."

I grabbed it and poured the contents over my head.

After grumbling for days on end about the rainshowers I'd been greeted with on arriving in France, I was now praying that the weather would turn back to that. You could have handed me a bottle of mayonnaise and I'd have tried pouring it over myself. The LCD display below the McDonalds sign now read 37 degrees Celsius.

"How much further do I have left?"

Andrew threw me a fresh towel and spread the crumpled map across the car bonnet.

"You're not even half way," he said, pointing at our location of Le Muy and attempting unsuccessfully to stifle a laugh while he took another slurp from the super-sized Coke he'd just bought for himself. "Probably about 70-odd miles to go."

If I hadn't been two weeks (and over 1400 miles) in, I would have quit there and then.

This heat was torture. Cycling seventy miles on an exercise bike in a sauna would have been preferable. To be honest, the main reason I hopped on my bike at all after devouring my ice-cream and lathering on another coat of sun cream was because it was genuinely more comfortable cycling into the breeze than it was standing in the frying pan that was McDonalds' car park. Dad sat quietly in the driver's seat of the car with a packet of Chicken McNuggets as I pedalled off, having a moment of quiet reflection after being flashed by the speed camera coming through the village. His imminent ninety Euro speeding fine had guaranteed not only a dent in his pride but also a healthy dose of bickering from Mum on their journey home the next day.

I made it through the remainder of the afternoon by locking into a subconscious metronomic rhythm. Cycle ten miles, re-fill water bottles at the nearest café/service station/tap/ditch, and then repeat. My family had long since gone ahead to our campsite in Aix-en-Provence as the chill of early evening began to set in. The rapid change in temperature forced me to throw on three extra layers, and the previously refreshing wind had now morphed into a head-on barrier to progress and fought to drive me back with every pedal stroke I took.

Glancing at the map what seemed like every minute, I tried to calculate if there was even enough time left in the day for me to reach Aix. The sun was on the cusp of dropping below the horizon, the sky had turned a dusky bluish-grey, and the headwinds had reached a whole new level of bananas where I had to stand out of my saddle just to move forward along flat stretches of road. It was like I'd been trapped in a wind tunnel. There were still twenty-five miles for me to cover, and I knew it wasn't safe, but all I could do was keep moving. Or trying to at least. Cycle now, think later.

Another hour passed and it was almost pitch black. I was still tiddling along a busy road with no front light and a sorry, slowly dying back light. A text message I'd been sent that morning by a friend back home reminding me to "Keep her between the hedges" popped into my mind. I was completely wiped. My legs had nothing left to give, I couldn't even see my handlebars anymore, and I was rapidly growing tired of guessing where the roadside ditch to my right was.

On finally arriving under the warm glow of the campsite lights to the east of Aix, I was reunited with the Collins crew and we trudged wearily towards our caravan. It felt like the longest walk of my life. I've been whacked out from sleep deprivation many times before, but I'd never experienced tiredness like this. My head was spinning from a combination of heat exhaustion and hunger. A few hundred metres from the caravan, I finally reached breaking point. I couldn't lift the weight of my legs any longer and physically curled up in a ball on the cold ground. As Dad picked me up and threw my arm over his shoulder, I vaguely remember mumbling "It'll be easier tomorrow" as he diligently carried his deadweight lump of a son towards a hot bowl of pasta and the cushioned embrace of the sofa bed in our caravan.

Up to my knees in dirty floodwater, my arm muscles groaned under the weight of the bike hoisted above my head. The German family cycling the other way who had kindly encouraged me to turn around and find another route to Lyon clearly didn't realise what I can be like when I set my mind on something. The River Rhone had burst its banks, and I was far too stubborn to retrace my journey to find a new path.

So far that day, my means of navigation had consisted purely of following the course of this roaring river and a bit of dampness around the ankles wasn't going to change that. Having already trekked once across the swamp to drop luggage on the other side of the floodwater, I took hold of my bike feeling like a character in one of those riddles your Maths teacher threw at you at school. Where a farmer has to shift a fox, a chicken and a bag of grain across a river? Well here I was playing the role of the hapless farmer, only with a bike, three pannier bags and a pair of beaten-up cycling shoes.

Rolling out of Aix-en-Provence the morning before, I had spent the vast majority of my jaunt up to Montélimar cycling through fields of olive trees flapping in the mistral winds. I'm informed that there are three and a half million olive trees in Provence. That's a lot. Especially when you consider that I have only ever met two people who like olives, and I'm pretty sure both of them were just pretending to like them to try and look cultured. The little, black monsters are the most heinous crime ever committed against the food world. They have no redeeming features. I longed to shout to the farmers, "You realise that you're doing all this work just for people to pick them off pizzas and chuck them in the bin?"

Montélimar wasn't exactly a hot spot for Airbnb room rental, meaning my only option for accommodation was a high-rise inner city hotel. And just my luck, the only rooms going were on the seventh floor. It had gone nine o'clock at the end of another hellish day into gusting north-westerly winds and I was desperate for a mattress of any description to collapse face-first onto. The receptionist clearly didn't care.

"Non, you can most definitely not store zat thing in here, sir."

"Could I not put it behind your desk until the morning?" I suggested.

"Eeuuuuggghhhhh! Absolutely not. Eet is feelthy."

"Well where am I supposed to store it then?"

"Outside. Not in here. Zis hotel is for people, not vehicles!"

"Somebody could steal parts off it though. Do you realise I need this bike to get home?"

"Zat is not my problem, sir."

I can't remember the last time I had such a passionate dislike for someone addressing me as "Sir". I turned around, my room key clasped in my hand, and wheeled my poor, unloved bike towards the main entrance. With one hand on the glass door opening into the harsh chill of the evening, I checked over my shoulder and saw my receptionist friend deeply engaged in dealings with the next customer/victim in the queue. The lift was roughly ten metres from where I was standing. I knew I had to time this to perfection.

Staring intently at the doors of the lift, the bell chimed to indicate it had arrived on the ground floor. Taking one final sideways glance back to reception to check the coast was clear, I watched the doors part and a young couple step out into the lobby. Trying to move quickly enough to get inside within the allocated time, but slowly enough not to draw attention to myself, I lunged inside just before the steel doors closed behind me. My bike squeezed in diagonally without a centimetre to spare.

The floor numbers on the screen ticked up painfully slowly. 2...3...4...then nothing.

Disaster. They must have seen me on CCTV. As the lift shuddered to a halt, I prepared myself to see the Wicked Receptionist of the West, ready to drag me down the staircase by my ear and throw Finn in a heap behind me. The doors parted and a tiny, elderly French lady, staying in the hotel and most probably just looking to go downstairs for dinner, stood awestruck.

"Pardon madame. C'est mon vélo. C'est très grande."

She smiled back, as if to say she was happy to accept my apology for filling the lift with my cargo. Either that or she was just a confused old lady. One way or the other, I couldn't think of the French for "Don't tell anyone", so I pressed the 'Close Doors' button, waved heartily at her and sped on towards Level 7.

Twelve hours later, after a glorious night's sleep, I sneaked my contraband out the front door and made my way for the banks of the Rhone. Within the first hour, I stumbled across two ladies from Switzerland on touring bikes down by the riverside. I knew that's where they were from because of the two miniature flags dangling off the back of their bikes. Moving along purposefully with thick-fleeced coats on their backs and weighed down by pannier bags of their own, I could see that they weren't just going for their morning groceries.

"We're cycling to Paris for our second match against Romania. We can't wait! We won our first match, you see."

They didn't look like your typical football fans, but their English was fantastic.

"Where have you cycled from?" I asked.

"From the south coast," replied the louder one of the pair. "This is the only game we were able to get tickets for, but it's so exciting. I can't remember the last time we had a team so strong. This is the most important game for Switzerland in years."

We rode together for half an hour before I realised I would never reach Lyon going at their tempo. Now I love a long, slow cycle just as much as the next person. But with arriving in Lyon that evening an absolute must ahead of the second Northern Ireland match with Ukraine, I couldn't afford a whole day tootling along at granny pace with a couple of fifty-something Roger Federer fanatics. We said our goodbyes, and I ratcheted up the pace to get back on course.

Until the flood, that is, thirty miles further down the road.

I was always the last one picked for football at primary school.

For a child so obsessed with the sport, I remember spending hours at home practising free-kicks against the wall to ensure my schoolmates would eventually realise what I had to offer. Long evenings wrapping my foot around the leather of a well-worn blue and white Mitre football. But the following morning at breaktime, it would be me and Richard again. We were always the last two standing. It sometimes got to the point where I'd be the very last person without a team, and one captain would say "Sure you have Stephen, we've got enough already." I'd trundle across to the unlucky side who'd been landed with me, looking down at my feet each step of the way.

Even at that tender age though – I think I was eight at the time – I realised that knockbacks could be turned into opportunities. No-one ever volunteered to be goalkeeper, and so I started asking my friend Mark to practice dribbling the ball past me after school while I dived at his feet to smother it away from him. Both of us huge Manchester United fans, Mark tried to emulate Ryan Giggs while I gobbled up the ball à la Peter Schmeichel if it ever drifted more than a couple of inches from his feet. Within a few months, I was one of the first names picked in the playground every day – as a goalie.

Identifying obstacles and badgering away to overcome them is something that still drives me on today just as much as it did when I was a shy schoolboy. And I couldn't help but feel a slightly heroic buzz that afternoon as I sat pulling my socks back on having reached dry land on the other side of the floodwater, my bike and pannier bags safely by my side.

I hadn't moved that much further down the path when another group of cyclists appeared ahead. Again, not your typical Sunday morning lycra-clad chain gang. Flags poked out – like my Swiss friends before them – from pannier bags on the back of their bikes, but this time it was the cross of St George flapping in the wind. The three young lads sitting on the bikes displayed a skin tone that suggested this wasn't their natural habitat. One was sporting a bright yellow wife-beater, while another stood bare-chested with the look of a man who'd been trapped in a tanning salon for a week and had just about crawled out alive.

"Are you boys from England?" I shouted over to them.

The tallest of the trio lifted his head up from his map and turned towards me.

"Yeah we are, mate, how's it going?" he replied in a surprisingly polished Yorkshire accent. "Good to meet you. You cycling to one of the games too?"

"I'm following the Northern Ireland boys around."

"Does that mean you're going to the Ukraine game in Lyon then?"

"That's where I'm headed right now."

The other two members of the cycling Barmy Army glanced at one another.

"No way, we're going to that match!" chimed Yellow Vest Boy.

"Seriously? You'll have the time of your life with our fans."

The Sheffield boys making all the noise

I've always felt like it is a duty of mine to enlighten outsiders on the magic of Northern Ireland that never makes it onto the telly. Instead of the dull-as-dishwater news coverage of amateur politicians disagreeing on a daily basis, there are five billion other amazing things that our broadcasters should be showing off.

We're the country who built the Titanic, for goodness sake (before the English sank it). We gave the sporting world George Best, Mary Peters and Dennis Taylor. We gave the music world Van Morrison, Snow Patrol and The Undertones. We've got a truck-load of hexagonal stones that were put there by a real-life giant. Our much-renowned Ulster Fry makes the Full English look so paltry and breadless it's embarrassing. And we're the only place on earth where you can get away with eating a crisp sandwich overflowing with Tayto Cheese and Onion for your lunch. Trust me, tasting is believing.

And when it comes to football, honorary supporters are always welcome with open arms. My three new friends – Joe, Stanley and Ben – couldn't have landed a better big match ticket. I knew the atmosphere at this one would be on a different level.

"Have you been to any other matches?" I asked them.

"Just the England one a few days back. Down in Marseille."

Oh. That one.

Not a game where the travelling English covered themselves in glory. Shameful images of rioting prior to the match harked back to the darkest days of hooliganism that plagued English football in the 1970's and 80's, with Russia's late equaliser sparking further humiliating scenes in the stands. In total, three days of violence rumbled on before and after England's opener, with tear gas sprayed liberally by police to stop self-professed 'ultras' from kicking lumps out of one another. As I completed the final descent into Nice on my bike, I had received texts from friends and family checking if I was safe, with pictures from Marseille all that was being beamed into their living rooms in terms of football coverage.

And that's the problem with idiots. It doesn't take many of them to give lots of very good people a very bad name.

These three didn't look or sound like hooligans though.

As the sunset cast its light over the river's surface, we shared embarrassing university stories, we placed bets on how far our respective teams would get in the tournament and we tunelessly sang football chants as they echoed down the now almost-deserted cycle path.

Despite my best efforts to convince them to stick with me until Lyon, they peeled off as we passed St Etienne. Forty miles short of my target for the evening, it took every shred of motivation left in my system not to turn in early and join them. Especially considering I'd intended to stop in St Etienne, until I saw a handful of messages on my phone. Two close friends from home – Jonny and Big Wes – had just touched base in Lyon and were insisting on my company that evening. If they had flown from Belfast to see me the night before the game, I suppose the very least I could do was cycle an extra forty miles in the cool haze of early evening.

Shaking hands and saying farewell to the newly-established Sheffield branch of the Northern Ireland Supporters Club, I started pumping my legs again in whichever direction the Rhone swept. As with many big cities, navigation gets substantially more testing the closer you get to the outskirts. Signs to the city centre carried me away from the course of the river and the magnificent ViaRhona cycle path which I had been leaning on for my sense of direction for most of the day.

Half past nine came and went. That was the time I'd told Jonny and Wes to wait for my triumphant arrival into the main square in Lyon's city centre. And yet I was meandering around the industrial suburbs, looking for a way in. Multiple options messed with my head at every junction I came to. Each one appeared to be taking me off in a wild tangent from where I wanted to go. Once again, light was dropping like a lead balloon. A sign appeared on my right hand side alerting me to the fact that I was still ten kilometres from the centre.

"Wes, I'm doing my best here, honest!" I shouted down the phone line, conscious that it was now a quarter past ten, the drizzle in the sky had started to turn nasty and I couldn't see any immediate access to the city on the horizon. Saying that, I couldn't see much. I was now squinting to make out what lay a matter of metres in front of me. I don't know which bothered me more. The darkness closing around me or the ferocious rain leaving me drenched, cold and disorientated and staring at a soggy, slowly disintegrating map.

I hung up half a minute later and switched off my phone to conserve the 2% of battery I had left, in case of emergency. I crossed two more junctions thick with late-night traffic. Another foolish cyclist became visible a few hundred metres up ahead, the red of his back light flashing through the downpour. I accelerated to catch him, and asked if he could suggest a route to the city centre.

This gentleman – called Marcel – was a Lyon native. He was making his way home after a long cycle that afternoon, as part of training for his own marathon Alpine cycling tour later that summer. In mercifully competent English, he invited me to stick to his tail while he cycled back to his flat in the centre of Lyon. Only in hindsight do I realise just how scuppered I would have been if I hadn't caught sight of him. We sped through tunnels, down narrow alleyways and across deserted parks for over twenty minutes until Marcel's bike-taxi service left me off at a lonely stone bridge in the heart of Lyon's old town.

Rain drummed down on my cheap helmet with ever-increasing volume. As Marcel disappeared around the corner to head home, I propped my bike against a lamppost and tried to make sense of the strange urban landscape I'd landed in. I wondered to myself where on earth I would go from here to try and find the boys.

And then a noise suddenly made me freeze to the spot where I stood. It sounded like the roar of thunder. A low rumble rang through the air. I listened more closely and it dawned on me that it wasn't thunder. There was a melody to it.

I grabbed my bike and followed the noise to the other side of the bridge. A smile broke out across my face as I began to make out familiar words and tunes. No longer was this a faint murmur, as I walked towards it, but a deafening anthem ringing out across the city. Breaking into a jog, I skipped past one more block of buildings pushing my bike as I went. It was unmistakeable now. The sound of wild laughter and cheering danced through the night sky. I turned one last corner and what I saw stopped me in my tracks.

Thousands of them. Everywhere you looked. Green and white shirts illuminated by streetlights around this grassy city centre park (that was fast turning into a mudbath). Groups of friends wearing berets and fake onions posed for photos in the driving rain beside the huge eight-foot tall EURO 2016 logo. Nobody was taking shelter from the elements. The heavens had opened, but I couldn't see one single person that cared.

The Nice campsite welcome was special for a number of reasons, but that was only a gathering of fifty people at best. This scene in Lyon was on a different scale. Northern Ireland supporters, young and old, were indulging in the biggest outdoor party I'd witnessed in my life. It felt like all the nervous tension before our first game had lifted with that opening defeat, and people were now intent on enjoying every last second of what small amount of time we might have left in France.

I took out my phone to record the dream-like scenes around me, when I was nearly wiped out altogether by someone leaping onto my back.

"Steeeeeeeeeevvvveeeee!"

Soaked to the skin with Wes (L) and Jonny (R) after landing in Lyon

Jonny shook the top of my helmet, slapped me on the back and shouted across to Wes on the other side of the park.

"I've found him! Here he is!"

Wes came bounding across moments later, much more sensibly kitted out for the weather. Jonny was wearing nothing but a t-shirt emblazoned with the letters 'GAWA' that now clung to him like a cheap tea-towel in the rain.

We looked like drowned rats, but felt like royalty. The three of us joined the masses for an obligatory sing-a-long before snapping up a handful of very welcome kebabs and making tracks towards our pad for the night. We never actually met our host Dylan, and considering the state we left his apartment in with our takeaway boxes, filthy footprints and empty Orangina bottles, that's probably not a bad thing. Big Wes wasted no time in claiming the solitary bunk bed in the flat, leaving me and Jonny to snuggle up together on a sofa-bed mattress on the cold floor beneath him.

"Stop your whining down there Stevo," piped Wes. "Nobody asked you to cycle here."

"Cheers, Wes. Appreciate it."

"Tell you what, that plane was pure luxury, wasn't it Jonny? Great view too."

Extremely proud of his razor-sharp wit, he chuckled as he turned over in his bed above our heads, and was snoring like a traction engine within less than a minute.

I woke up with a jolt.

Deafening, tinny music burst through the silence from somewhere on the other side of Dylan's room. My eyes were unbearably heavy. There was no way it was morning yet.

"The day has arrived gentlemen," bellowed Jonny in his finest town-crier voice, "the glorious day when our boys in green and white will become heroes forever," temporarily turning down the volume on his handmade Northern Ireland playlist to deliver his rousing speech to the people.

"Shut up, you banty!" shouted Wes, chucking a pillow at him and promptly going back to sleep.

I grabbed a brioche from the half-eaten bag beside my mattress, and lobbed a second one in the direction of Jonny.

"Carry on, I'm listening," I yawned as I propped a folded pillow behind my tired head. "Inspire me, captain."

Jonny nodded approvingly and picked up where he had left off, draped in a sarong fashioned out of his NI flag. "Hundreds of painstaking hours on the training pitch have been boiling down to these ninety minutes for our warriors." It was hard to take anything he was saying seriously with the stirring soundtrack of '*Will Grigg's on Fire*' (the techno remix) blaring from his iPod in the background. "Not since before the three of us were born have our brave countrymen had this kind of opportunity to shine on the biggest stage. And we're ready to grab it with both hands. We're ready to see a nation's dreams come true. We're ready to make history, aren't we boys?"

"Mm-hmm, that's right" I muttered, fighting desperately to hold my eyes open.

"I said…AREN'T WE BOYS?"

"Yes, Jonny, of course we are. Sorry, YES!"

In between Jonny's overblown, patriotic prose, I could hear playful sniggering from the top bunk above my head. I craned my neck to look upwards.

"Wes, what are you doing up there?"

"Hee hee heeeeeeeee!" came the childish response.

"Wes…?"

"You know what Stevo? Being married is *class*," he crowed. "You should try it."

"Ah, I see. Has the Mrs been sending you messages again?"

"Ohhhhh yes," chuckled the big man. "Can't beat it. We need to find you a wee Lyon woman. Spotted any suitable candidates for him yet, Jonny boy?"

"What about that doll from the bakery round the corner?"

"Ooh la la! You know what, you might be on to something. She could be the one. Stevo, you fancy going round and getting some croissants for the lads?"

"Oui oui!" echoed Jonny. "And don't forget to say 'Merci beaucoup' and 'avez vous une numero téléphone, mon cherie?' while you're there!"

Like two schoolgirls who'd been let loose for the week. Married life changes people in different ways, but you could sense the emotional release in the boys being unchained for a few brief days off grid. Having all left school together in 2006, Wes was first to bite the dust and get hitched back in 2013, before Jonny followed suit a year later.

The three of us have ventured on annual camping holidays for the past five years (we're in the long-term process of spending a weekend in a tent, one year at a time, in each of the twenty-six counties of the Republic of Ireland), but this French extravaganza was by far our most eagerly-anticipated holiday yet.

"Seriously though, Steve, what do you think about when you're on your bike all day?" asked Jonny.

"Well we know who he'll be thinking about from this point on, after his visit to the boulangerie," chimed Wes. "Isn't that right, Romeo?"

I have no idea how the two of them found wives.

"No, but I mean it," added Jonny. "I get bored going cycling for half an hour in the evening after work. What do you actually think about for ten hours a day out here?"

It was a great question. For once in my life, I didn't have an answer. I hadn't stopped at any stage on my trip and thought about my thoughts.

"One difference is that there's slightly more visual stimulation in the French Alps than the outskirts of Ballymena," I started. "But in all honesty, I don't know."

Two hours after breakfast, a very different scene lay before us.

We could barely see each other's faces in the frighteningly dark room, as the bearded man's lifeless body lay propped up by a cold, brick wall.

There was nothing left that we could think to do. We'd exhausted all options. Every new, unexpected noise made us jump. Frantically rummaging through filthy rags in the pitch black with only my phone light to guide us, I was beginning to despair when Wes cried out from the other side of the windowless dungeon.

"I think I've found it!"

We'd been given far more tips by the member of staff watching on the hidden camera than we should have been allowed, but finally the key to the treasure chest was in our grasp. I don't imagine too many Northern Irish football fans were spending the hours leading up to kick-off trapped in an escape room down a back-alley in Lyon's city centre. We enjoy doing things in an unconventional manner.

We first discovered this curiously addictive pastime on the away trip to Bucharest during the qualifying campaign. Romania had defeated us 2-0 on that particular trans-European mission, but one of the highlights of the trip had been stumbling across the phenomenon of being locked in a dark room containing a bizarre assortment of household objects and cryptic clues, and having an hour to find your way out.

The unorthodox appeal might be slightly less apparent if more places like it started opening back home. Imagine a solid, heavy-handed Belfast man slamming a door behind you down a back street while growling "Good luck gittin outta that wan nigh, and 'member I'll be watching yous", before leaving you quivering in a dark room with no windows and no heating.

Maybe we'll just save it for trips abroad.

The subway train was rocking. The noise intensified with each new batch of poor, unsuspecting locals that stepped on board. Jonny had dragged us through the heaving green and white multitude to the front window of the train carriage, so he could drape his Northern Ireland flag across the windscreen and make it clear to every approaching station that we were very much in town. The assembled choir (reasonably well lubricated with cheap French beer by now) were in full flow, and showed no signs of stopping.

"Yoooooouuuuu are my Daaaaaaavis, my Stevie Davis…"

Their tuneless, joy-filled words rang over the din of plastic windows being hammered to within an inch of their breaking point. Cultured French girls along the sides of the carriage looked up from romantic novels and grasped their handbags slightly tighter than normal. Shuffling awkwardly in their seats, they tried their utmost to pretend that they were oblivious to the scenes around them. Like when Londoners look absolutely everywhere else possible on the tube before dreaming of locking eyes with another human being. Eventually, one elegant young student couldn't fight it any longer and cracked a smile as our ever-growing crowd gathered in unison to belt out '*Can't Take My Eyes Off You*' in her direction.

Disembarking at Place Bellecour, we were swept along by the tide of people in the direction of the snaking queue for the free matchday bus service. The churning wheels that would carry us on the final leg of our journey to the Stade de Lyon. The sun stood high in the afternoon sky, as fans in replica kits and sunglasses clambered on top of the 'EURO 2016' letters at the fan zone. We partook in a spot of C-list celebrity spotting, even managing to grab a chat in the shade with Mark Simpson from BBC Northern Ireland. Slightly amusing how starstruck we became in the presence of a local newsreader.

As we strolled back towards the boisterous all-singing and dancing queue weaving its way around the square, one voice piped up suddenly above the general hum of noise.

"Big Steve! It's the man himself!"

There's nothing like seeing the ugly mug of an old friend after too much time spent apart.

The first Northern Ireland match I ever attended was a 5-0 home defeat to Spain. Thirteen years old at the time, I'd been invited by Nellie, a friend I'd met on the school bus. His dad, Dessie, drove the two of us down after class finished, arriving just in time to take our seats in the family enclosure at Windsor Park. A typically chilly Belfast evening awaited and I remember being buried under layers of Adidas tracksuit tops. I also remember the Spaniards being absolutely scintillating. Wave after wave of attack tormented our awestruck home defence with the Real Madrid legend, Raúl, at the peak of his powers.

Sixteen years later, that night in April 2002 remains the root cause of my love for Northern Ireland's footballing endeavours. And it all started with our lads getting walloped.

Over the years at secondary school, I went to many more NI games as a result of Dessie's generosity, not only providing tickets, but ferrying us on the two-hour round trip, giving us snacks for the road and always reliably being the one, solitary person in the stadium showing any manner of restraint on the very rare occasions that we managed to score a goal – "Focus! Come on lads, switch on again! He's clean through!"

Dessie even gave up his ticket for the famous England match in 2005 to allow me in. The most sought-after home ticket in a generation, and he sacrificed his spot in the crowd for one of his boy's mates. If he hadn't allowed me a glimpse into this magical side of Northern Irish sporting culture, I would never have found myself soaking up magical days out like the one now before me.

"Nellie, no way! How's it going?"

"Steve, you beautiful, beautiful man. So excited to be here. This is dreamland!"

"When did you arrive?"

"Flew into Paris from Philadelphia a couple of nights ago. Bit tired, but wouldn't have missed it for the world."

"And hang on…it isn't? Dessie!"

With Nice and now these scenes in Lyon, each game was starting to feel like one massive reunion. A huge coming together of old faces that Northern Ireland games over the years had introduced me to, and many others besides who I would never have guessed had a passing interest in football. To be fair, most of them probably didn't, but who cares? This was one party that no-one from our little corner of the British Isles, football fan or not, wanted to miss out on.

I don't know the man or woman who designed the Stade de Lyon, but they must have encountered difficulties getting planning permission anywhere near the city. It wouldn't surprise me if you told me it was built by the same team who choose the airports that Ryanair fly to. "What's that, sir? You'd like to go to Stockholm? Of course we can help. Allow us to fly you to some barren, long-forgotten wasteland fifty miles away from there. You're very welcome."

After travelling with the sweaty flock of fans via tube, tram and bus, we finally arrived at the gladiatorial arena inside which our warriors sat primed for battle. Those same young men who normally ply their trade in the lower lurches of English and Scottish league football before scanty crowds of a few hundred punters. We boast a small handful who hold their own for teams in the English Premier League, but there was nobody in our starting line-up for whom this was not the most important ninety minutes of their footballing lives.

Filtering through security checks with fans bringing out the oldest gags in the book – "Careful what you're doing down there, I'm a married man you know" – we stepped onto the vast concourse outside the ground. The green and white of our supporters blended seamlessly into the ever-growing crowd of yellow and blue backing our opponents. Posing for group photos, buying drinks for strangers they'd never met before, and having face paint of the Ukrainian colours slapped on their cheeks, it was a spectacular carnival of everything that is right about the beautiful game.

Just as Jonny and I were flicking on the charm at the fast food counter to try and get discount on our hot dogs, I heard a strangely familiar voice.

"Is that Cauliflower over there?"

Mark – the same one I grew up sharing long evenings of football with back in our younger days – stood sporting an outrageous pair of bright green sunglasses and a red hand of Ulster wrapped around his shoulders, his long-suffering wife by his side. The name he gives me – and he remains the only person alive to call me it – is the result of a church group paying a visit to our primary school when we were six years old, and teaching us a harvest song called 'Cauliflowers Fluffy and Cabbages Green'. The second Mark realised this sounded vaguely like my surname, the song became my theme tune in the playground.

"Can't believe you went and made it here, boy," he said as we brought it in for a man-sized embrace, the "boy" at the end of his sentence pronounced "bye" and a footnote to almost every sentence he ever says.

With our Ukrainian brothers pre-match outside the Stade de Lyon

A few minutes later, I saw a couple who sit in the same row as me at home games back in Belfast. A man I'd got chatting to on the train into Nice for the previous match appeared out of nowhere and threw his arms around me. Three lads I hadn't seen since getting the bus with them over a decade ago came to say hello. Everyone was there.

The atmosphere crackled from the second we walked out into the stand.

Without being able to find three seats together when we applied for tickets, Jonny and I shuffled towards the very bottom of the lowest tier, while Wes took his perch higher up in the gods. At no point before the game, however, did Jonny and I imagine that our seats were going to be the very front row. Tucked beside the corner flag of the goal Northern Ireland would attack in the second half, we couldn't have asked for a more perfect vantage point.

At times, the first half felt more like a rock concert than a football match. We were aware in the stands that there was a bit of sport going on in the background, but were mostly occupied being swept along by the tide of raucous singing and chanting, including a twenty-minute epic rendition of '*Will Grigg*'.

Ten minutes into the second half, jet-black clouds appeared over the stadium and a smattering of hailstones fell from the sky. These didn't relent, growing heavier and more stinging in nature as time went by, and within minutes you could see them trampoline off the playing surface. It wasn't exactly the Seventh Plague, but the referee decided that Northern Ireland were gaining too much of an unfair advantage from the rubbish weather and called all of the players down the tunnel.

"What the fudge?" shrieked Jonny. "It's only a few drops of rain!"

I should explain. Any time Jonny gets irate, his face goes a bright tomato shade of red and he starts liberally throwing around the F-word – fudge.

"We were battering them before he brought them in, this better not change things," I said.

"You're fudging right. If we lose this now, that ref's gonna have me to deal with. And he's not gonna like it!"

The bemused players were back in position ten minutes later. Their hair damp, their shirts sticking to them from the rainwater, but a steely fire still in their eyes. The concerns we'd had about the momentum shifting with the break in proceedings were quashed immediately. We were back on the front foot from the off.

Half-time in Lyon, our boys in the ascendancy

Soon, the only mumblings between deafening chants were from those anxious that we wouldn't translate this dominance into any end product. It is an age-old problem for us, after all. I vividly remember attending each home game during the spell in the early 2000's where we failed to score a goal for over fourteen games, giving rise to the fantastic Proclaimers parody – "I would wait 500 minutes, and I would wait 500 more, just to be the man who waits 1000 minutes to see our country score."

From our front row seats, and with Northern Ireland now attacking the goal we were standing behind, we were at the heart of the action. Noise levels reached a new crescendo every time a green shirt gained possession of the ball. The rain continued to hammer down, and pockets of fans in the lower tiers around the stadium ran for cover higher up in their stands, in what resembled a human Mexican-wave. All around the stadium except for our stand, that is. We weren't going anywhere.

I'd long since gone hoarse from singing. Jonny threw his arm around me and held his phone aloft to take a dripping-wet selfie of us just as we won a free-kick wide on the left. Behind us Ollie Norwood was placing the ball purposefully on the damp turf and signalling for bodies in the penalty box to make the runs they'd rehearsed for months on the training ground.

As Ollie stood with hands on hips preparing to sweep the ball goalwards, our fans broke into the '*Seven Nation Army*'-inspired chant of "Go, Gareth McAuley!" Few players in recent years have enjoyed G-Mac's popularity. Not far off being able to claim a free bus pass, he is more prolific now in his late-30's than most teenage frontmen are. He organises and galvanises players around him, and finds himself (incredibly) in the Top 10 all-time goalscorers list for Northern Ireland despite playing at centre-back. Simply by being such a mammoth presence at set-pieces, just like this one.

The crowd fell silent seconds before Ollie connected with the ball. So quiet you could hear the thud of the inside of his boot against the heavy leather. As the ball floated in slow-motion over the sea of yellow and green bodies in front of the goal, G-Mac pulled off a feat of gymnastic artistry the like of which you would normally only witness from a Russian fourteen-year old in a leotard. Leaping like a salmon at the back post, he arched his neck to direct the ball back across goal beyond the despairing reach of the Ukrainian goalkeeper and into the far corner of the net.

The next two minutes of my life were a blur.

I can't accurately tell you what happened in the aftermath of that goal. Sheer frenzy broke out amongst 20,000 delirious fans around and behind me.

I remember screaming. There was a lot of that.

I also remember sprinting up the narrow steps in our stand to the very top row of seats before haring back down again, hugging and kissing any individual who dared set foot in my path. I didn't know who or where I was. By the time I'd made it back to Jonny in the front row, the players had flopped on top of one another in a gigantic pile-on right in front of us. We loudly declared our undying love to G-Mac as he stood up, raising his arms to his legion of followers and kissing the badge on his shirt.

From that moment on, it was party time. Like never before.

We deserved to be in front, there was no question about that, but we had never once imagined how good it might feel. The team's build-up to the tournament had been based heavily around the slogan 'Dare to Dream', but I don't think anybody realised dreamland might be as euphoric as this.

I had always maintained that nothing would eclipse David Healy's goal to defeat England in 2005, but this was a whole new level of incredible. This actually meant something. If we could hold onto this lead, we could start seriously thinking about qualifying for the knock-out stages of the competition. The players kept their feet firmly on the gas, up until the dying moments when the fourth official indicated six minutes of added time. Please don't throw this away lads, we pleaded.

Entering the dying moments, the ball fell to my favourite player, Josh Magennis, close to the corner flag on the right of the pitch.

"The corner, Josh! Take it to the corner!"

The same shriek rang out from just about everyone in our stand, desperate for the big man to use his strength and stubbornness to wind down the clock without forfeiting possession.

Only Josh knows why he decided to drop his shoulder and cut inside, but it was one of the most sublime pieces of skill under pressure I've ever seen. Especially from someone not renowned for his delicate footwork. He dashed for the by-line before cutting it back into the danger area. Steve Davis met the cross, and when his shot could only be parried by the flailing arms of the keeper, Niall McGinn was on the prowl like a sniffer dog at a music festival to tuck away the rebound.

The reaction from our manager, Michael O'Neill, was beautiful. Only on TV footage later that evening did I fully appreciate the relief that howled from his face as he sank to his knees in jubilation. I climbed onto the four-foot wall in front of our seats, and stood with arms aloft like a heavyweight prizefighter, before losing balance in the midst of my own excitement and spraining my right ankle on landing. It didn't phase me in the least. Ecstatic scenes continued for an hour after the final whistle sounded. It was the perfect ending to a magical game of football.

*Scenes in our end after Niall made it 2-0 –
me 2nd from the left (Photo: The Sun)*

Dancing arm in arm with new friends of all ages, we located an equally-jubilant Wes and the three of us took an age before eventually meandering out of the ground.

Wes turned to me as we loitered on the concourse outside the stadium, and said "What about the exam results then Stevo?"

Of course.

I'd refused to check all day. After six years of toiling through medical school, including countless occasions where I was inches from packing it in altogether because of pathetic end of year reports and demeaning consultants, the results of my finals had been released that morning. I'd promised the lads I wouldn't ruin our day by checking for bad news before kick-off.

But with a famous victory now under our collective belts, I realised this might be the last internet access I'd have for the next twenty-four hours at least. I split from the other two and asked the stewards if they'd allow me back into the stands for five minutes. With the seats now almost entirely empty around the Stade de

Lyon, I took a pew directly behind the net that our two goals had flown into, three rows back from the pitch.

Taking a deep breath, I logged onto the stadium wifi and watched as my cheap phone laboured to access my university email account. Half a minute passed before an Excel spreadsheet popped up, scattered with confusing numbers. I glanced upwards where groundsmen in their fluorescent orange jackets were poking and prodding the weary turf, already preparing it for the next game. I scrolled down beyond the irrelevant figures and percentages until my eyes landed on two words in the bottom-right corner of the screen.

Outcome: Pass.

I lifted my head and smiled. A grin etched firmly across my face, I strode towards the lads, who were looking nervously back at me.

Jonny could tell from my expression alone, charging towards me as he leapt onto my shoulders screaming "Dr Collins is in the building!"

Our Northern Ireland heroes had snatched the most monumental win, and I was now a fully-qualified doctor. All in the same day. The scale of it all was starting to hit home.

Oh fudge.

Surrounded by grass-munching cattle struggling to stand upright in the driving winds, I had landed back to the hum-drum normality of cycle touring with a thump. Having grown up beside a dairy farm, I had a vague recollection of my old neighbours chatting about the Charollais breed. Or 'Charlie' as they pronounced it in the wilds of County Armagh. Imposing golden-brown creatures, commonly seen on postcard pictures with bells draped from their necks. As I slugged down a mouthful of lukewarm Fanta and gasped to regain my breath following another painfully undulating chunk of countryside, an army of them stood gawping at me and chewing. And then chewing a little bit more.

Celebrations the previous night had carried on into the wee, small hours, as Wes, Jonny and I partied with a horde of revellers at the unofficial fanzone. Established and now seemingly owned by the Northern Irish travelling contingent, this patch of urban space that I'd unwittingly staggered upon on arrival in Lyon was heaving post-match with jubilant men, women and children. Right through the night, locals were treated to ecstatic, tone-deaf chants and more dodgy dancing than you'd see at a Hugo Duncan outside broadcast.

Now less than twenty-four hours later, while our heroic players were no doubt enjoying ice baths and extended massage sessions, I was rediscovering the delight of uphill treks into shuddering headwinds, with my rear end hovering an inch above my bike seat to avoid pressing deeper into the saddle sores that coated the finer points of my derrière. My knuckles gleamed white as I clung on to the handlebars in the face of raging gales blowing through the sparse grassy plains.

Before ploughing through Charolles, I had spent the morning taking the rare opportunity to share time with supporters going about their business at campsites in the sprawling suburbs of Lyon. With my enforced schedule of only taking rest days on matchdays, I had accepted prior to my travels that I'd have to miss a lot of the casual holiday banter that the wider family of fans would be soaking up. But turning my wheels under the high early morning sun, I stopped every five minutes or so to talk to any groups that I managed to spot on the roadside wearing green or white regalia. We hugged, we laughed, we mocked each other's borderline life-threatening sunburn, and shared croissants together from cheap multipacks.

Twenty-five miles north of Lyon, long after I'd left the travelling Northern Irish fans behind, I noted an oddly familiar sight. All of a sudden I wasn't sure where I was anymore. Almost crashing into an elderly couple at a zebra crossing as I craned my neck upwards, I freewheeled into Saint Georges de Reneins surprised, amused and overjoyed in equal measure at what I saw.

At the heart of Burgundy's Beaujolais region, I wasn't the only thing flapping in the wind. I had to do a double-take (and then a triple-take) at the sight of Northern Ireland flags flying proudly atop every lamppost in the tiny medieval village. Flags (or "flegs") are a slightly bizarre phenomenon in our neck of the woods, and generate debate and controversy like very little else in Northern Ireland. Streets wanting to identify themselves as nationalist areas will hang Irish tricolours from every available lamppost. At the same time, unionist estates claim their territory and allegiance to the rest of the UK with the red, white and blue of the Union flag. It's been decades since the primary function of our lampposts was to provide light on dark evenings.

It felt like I'd taken a wrong turn and arrived at the hill leading up to my house in Coleraine. Every lamppost was adorned. But on this occasion, a new identity was being claimed. The Ulster flag (the emblem most closely associated with Northern Ireland) appeared alternating with green flags plastered with the words 'Green and White Army'. There are many things I adore about Michael

O'Neill, but arguably the most significant thing he has achieved as our manager is successfully forging a new national pride within the fanbase of being Northern Irish first and foremost, instead of feeling weighed down by the never-ending 'British or Irish' debate.

Still unsure of why this insignificant village was so taken with Northern Irish fanaticism, I navigated my way around the roundabout. A banner hung from the sign in the middle of the junction loudly stating "Welcome to the Northern Ireland Euro 2016 squad". Then it clicked. A feature I'd watched on BBC News NI before leaving home shot back into my mind about the luxurious country chateau in a non-descript village that our players and staff were planning to call home as their base in France. This was it.

Desperate for a momentary glimpse of the greatest sportsmen on earth, I slowed to snail pace. Surely finding a hotel in a place like this would be easy. Like finding a lorry in a car park. Or so I thought. Nothing but trees, fields and more trees. I began to wonder if Michael and his crew had been getting gardeners to plant hundreds of towering shrubs to obscure the hotel from public view. I did four laps of the village, but to no avail. Clearly a job as the Belfast Telegraph's paparazzi isn't on the horizon for me.

Surrounded by that night's dinner on the roads of Charolles

The cows appeared very soon after. In their droves. With tears streaming down my cheeks from gusts whipping around me in the now-overcast late afternoon, I stopped to photograph a particularly inquisitive small herd of cattle, rewarding them with a wodge of grass each for their trouble. Shivering through the front doors of my hotel after eight o'clock that evening, I scurried to the restaurant in my trackies. I scanned the menu handed to me by the bubbly waitress, and it was a no-brainer. Not without the occasional pang of guilt, I treated myself to one of our bovine friends for dinner. Medium to well done. The temptation was just too much after eight hours looking at their faces staring back at me.

I sliced through the tender meat with my steak knife, and just as I began to chew I caught sight through the window of an old, weathered Charollais cow standing on the other side of a barbed wire fence, looking back at me with the most unforgiving eyes I think I've ever seen.

The next day, and the sun shone brightly once more. The road stretched up ahead, rising towards a glimmering horizon.

Peeling off at the third exit of an impressively large roundabout, I flicked down a couple of gears and injected some acceleration. Occasionally glancing at the heat haze dancing on the road's smooth surface, I tried to focus on the white painted line that I was delicately poised on.

Then, just as I began to wonder why almost no traffic was travelling down such a hefty, open road, flashing red lights appeared in my line of vision to the left.

It was the boys in blue. Or les garcons in bleu, as people round this part of the world probably refer to them. To be fair, I was surprised – and quite proud – that it had taken almost three weeks on the road for me to have my first dealing with them.

"Eh! Arrête!"

I pressed the brakes and slid to a standstill on the gravelly hard-shoulder, their bellowing voices ringing out behind me.

"C'est interdit! C'est interdit!"

"Mon vélo, c'est bien ici?" I smiled and said with a cheeky glint in my eye – "It's OK here?"

"Non, c'est interdit!"

Forbidden. Could just about remember that word from French oral questions at school. Good thing as well, considering how much these lads loved using it. Once more, I felt flattered by their assumption that I understood what they were saying.

"Non non non, c'est bien," I uttered with confidence. "Ca n'est pas un autoroute."

Yes, that's right. I had now started telling the French police what was and what was not a motorway.

"Il y a un signal (road sign) dans le route," one of them barked angrily, pointing his index finger firmly back towards the roundabout I had come from. "C'est *interdit!*"

Saliva sprayed from the corners of my unhinged friend's mouth as his temper tantrum escalated, the tiny blood vessels on his forehead becoming more and more prominent with every sentence he shrieked. I hadn't seen any road signs. And even if I had, I hadn't understood their message. So surely that gives me the benefit of the doubt.

The shouty one looked over at his quieter colleague, who was standing by the open door of their police car with the sirens still flashing. They knew they were fighting a losing battle. Amateur cyclists don't come much tougher than this one, fellas. Or so I kept telling myself, as I knocked back a swig of orange juice and tried to conjure up another sentence from my diminishing mental storehouse of French vocabulary.

"C'est stupide!" I spluttered, shrugging my shoulders as I turned away from them. Literally the only thing that came to mind at that very moment. Again, in hindsight, probably not the smartest thing to say to two people who had the authority to imprison me in a foreign jail.

I hate when the law gets you in that smug, self-satisfying way. Yes, I know they're only doing their job, but if they could only try not to be so impossible to like while they do it. Like when you find a traffic warden gleefully scribbling a parking ticket just as you return to your car after popping into the supermarket. Or when you get a speeding fine at two o'clock in the morning because a police officer is hiding behind a bush instead of doing the decent thing and getting a night's sleep. Some people just don't help themselves.

The French fuzz said one or two other things in response to my concluding remarks, fairly animated things, but I could only understand a fraction and so I trudged on. Having been explicitly told not to cycle back, I walked slowly and uncomfortably for almost a mile back to the roundabout in my cleats. The sun scorched the skin on the back of my neck with every clunking step I took.

I turned and looked over my shoulder only to see their grinning faces beaming back at me, the two of them waving like schoolchildren who'd just downed ten packets of Haribo as they shouted "Bonne journée, monsieur!" in unison.

Fifteen minutes of walking on my heels later, I arrived back at the roundabout where it all began, and a pole rose out of the ground beside me. I staggered forward to read the other side of the sign and was greeted by a large picture of a bicycle with a red line through it. Tail firmly between my legs, I leapt on to my saddle and veered away from the motorway towards the quiet canal path on the other side of the road.

My vague plan had been to rest my head in Nevers, an ancient Roman town on the banks of the Loire. However, since being turfed off the motorway I had made surprisingly rapid progress along the tree-covered cycle paths on Nevers' outskirts. The sun hung high above the horizon, and to my estimation there was still a good two hours cycling left in the day.

Searching on my phone, I spotted a bed available in a family cottage in the relatively unknown village of Raveau, to the east of La Charité sur Loire. Not the sort of place that features prominently on your standard fold-out map of France but it was twenty miles closer to Paris and, while there was still light in the sky and power in my legs, that was good enough for me.

Spectacular countryside engulfed me on all sides as I pedalled into the sort of soft summer breeze that cyclists dream of. At one point, a startled deer skipped in front of me on the deserted roads leading through the forest canopy of Le Bois de Raveau. Before long, the most paltry of road signs welcomed me to Raveau itself, and it looked like fields were all that lay before me.

I stumbled around for half an hour asking local farmers if they'd heard of my host family, without success, before swallowing my pride and phoning for a lift. I perched myself on a grassy bank as the sun finally dropped out of sight, and gazed with my jaw plonked on the floor at the most magnificent purple sky glinting on corn fields and winding roads as far as the eye could see. Minutes later a mustard-yellow landrover chugged to a halt behind me, and I threw Finn into the boot.

Laurene, my host in Raveau, reached past her one-year old son in his highchair and offered me some jam to put on the crèpes we were enjoying for breakfast.

"C'est quelle sorte de confiture?" I asked in shambolic, thrown-together French.

"Aaah, c'est la confiture de prunes."

"Prunes?"

"Oui, prunes. Do you like them?"

Prunes are not high up the list of my favourite things in the world. In fact they're fairly close to the bottom. As far as I'm concerned, prunes are what you give constipated, old people to get their bowels firing. Not exactly what I want churned up in my jam in the morning. Especially before a long day in the saddle. The very last thing I needed was having to look for toilets in every village I passed through due to explosive prune-induced diarrhoea.

Even so, I was intrigued by the colour of what lay before me.

"I'm confused," I uttered, giving up on my French altogether. "Why's it red?"

"Because prunes are red." She shrugged her shoulders and laughed, looking at her husband as if to say 'Who let this nutter into our house?'

"Really? I've only ever seen black ones."

"Black? No! We would throw them straight into the bin if they were black."

"Have you got any red prunes in the house?" I asked. "I'd love to see one."

Prove it, darling. If you've got some weird, genetically-modified red prune, I want it brought to me as evidence.

"Yes, of course," smiled Laurene, shuffling away to a shadowed area in the far corner of her kitchen.

Returning half a minute later, she flung a small object in my direction, stating with great conviction, "There you go. A prune. A *red* prune."

I looked at the plum in my hands, and thought 'This girl has actually lost it.'

"This isn't a prune, this is a plum!"

"A palumma?" she replied.

"A plum. Plum. P-L-U-M."

"OK, but we call it a prune."

Of course you do. What a ludicrous language.

I don't like coffee. I think it's got to do with the horrendously pretentious people who drink it. For those of us who feel uncomfortable wearing checked shirts that are two sizes too small, growing patchy beards and pretending to prefer quinoa to steak and chips, coffee shop culture is never going to be up our street.

Which is strange for a cyclist to say. The two continue to go from strength to strength in their curious relationship with one another. Nowadays, anytime you drop in to a coffee shop for a brew on a Saturday lunchtime, you're guaranteed to bump into a small group of men squeezed into ill-fitting, retro-coloured cycling tops knocking back espressos with their eye-wateringly expensive carbon bikes perched next to them. Chatting about average speeds up their most recent hill climbs like they're sat looking out over the Dolomites, when in reality they're in a bleak industrial estate somewhere in County Antrim.

It was another quiet Sunday morning on the rolling roads of France, and once again I hadn't managed to scavenge any food the previous night. Going without an evening meal is a challenge for people like me at the best of times, but this problem becomes borderline catastrophic when you're offloading in the region of 5,000 calories each day on a bicycle and need something in reserve for when you crawl out of bed and pull on your sweat-tinged bib shorts again.

I was desperately short of energy. My legs were slowly grinding to a halt, and the tank was very nearly dry. The sugary prune jam from breakfast had long-since lost its effect. Perched on a park bench beside a water fountain in another non-descript town, I reached for my phone to check the time. It wasn't even noon and this was already my third break of the day. If you had placed a hundred flapjacks in front of me at that precise moment, I would have demolished every one of them. Back in the real world, however, I was down to my last two. And I knew they had to be rationed over the remainder of the day, with the country's shops lying in a Sabbath slumber once more.

As the sticky heat intensified throughout the afternoon, my breaks became more frequent. Stopping to fill my two well-worn bottles at the sight of anything that looked like it may contain water, I slogged right to the very brink of my breaking point along those weaving roads. For the first time in my whole journey, every mile felt like a mile. My mind started playing tricks on me. A road sign would appear telling me I had 15 kilometres until the next large town. Then, after what felt like half an hour of cycling I would stagger past another sign saying there were 14 kilometres to go. I hadn't just hit the proverbial wall – I had freewheeled headlong into it, and it felt like I was repeatedly thumping my head against it. I was mentally and physically spent.

The same pattern continued all afternoon. Stuttering from one village to the next and no further before making time for prolonged recovery and intense emotional therapy. I'd always viewed myself as a strong-willed individual, but this notion was now being seriously put to the test.

Just then, as it approached 6pm, I found quite possibly the only village in France with a café open on a Sunday. I did a double-take as my eyes caught sight of an open doorway with a small sign on the pavement outside, the thick smell of coffee permeating the air. Remember, I don't normally like coffee. But after eight hours of nothing but flapjacks and water, I was ready to spend like a Russian oil baron on payday.

I stepped into the dusty, deserted shop and asked for a cup of 'café'. I didn't realise at the time, but 'café' does not mean coffee. What you need to ask for is 'café au lait'. The 'with milk' bit is very, very important as it happens. If you plump for a straight-up 'café' when ordering beverages on the continent, you will be rewarded with an espresso of near-treacle consistency packaged into a miniature white cup.

Thomas, the custodian of this intriguing establishment, stood with his cigarette hanging from one side of his mouth as he listened to my order. Without removing the cigarette at any point during our conversation, he mumbled that I should take a seat outside and he'd bring it to me.

I slumped into the uncomfortable green plastic chair on the pavement, and looked out across the village square. Not a soul to be seen. No traffic on the roads and – with the exception of Thomas – no signs of human life. The thirty miles I still needed to cover before reaching my destination of Moret-sur-Loing, on the fringes of Fontainebleau, didn't even bear thinking about. I only just managed to muster the motivation to lift my head from the table when Thomas' voice chirped behind me through the cloud of smoke emanating from his mouth.

"Votre café, monsieur. Voila."

"M-m-merci beaucoup, Thomas" I stammered, my lips now beginning to tremble in the cool of the evening.

I was handed a tiny cup of what could only be described as pure rocket fuel. I'd never had an espresso before, and so I nonchalantly knocked it back in one, unsure of the proper etiquette. And holy smokes. I don't know what Thomas put in that cup, and I don't know if I want to, but it worked like a dream. You wouldn't get a caffeine hit like that if you injected the stuff straight into your veins. With my eyes lit up like beacons, out of nowhere I felt like I had the energy to run from Thomas' tiny café to Tokyo and back.

Shaking my head in disbelief and mild euphoria, I shrieked a quick goodbye in Thomas' direction, left him a five Euro tip and hopped on board my bike to start the home stretch. The remaining miles blazed by. Fatigue was a long-forgotten foe that had been swiftly conquered. I have no doubt in my mind that it was Thomas, and him alone, who carried me home that night, and I'm forever in his debt.

In Moret-sur-Loing that night, the motel that met me on arrival was so grimy I can still smell the stench in my nostrils just thinking about it. The cheapest place I could find by a long shot, and I could tell why as soon as I arrived.

Which was surprising considering how picturesque the rest of the town was. Strolling over the sandstone bridge into the walled marketplace as the sun went down was like stepping into an oil painting. In fact, a number of famous artists like Alfred Sisley and Vincent van Gogh chose to use the town as a subject for some of their most celebrated landscape paintings.

Leaving the glistening river behind me, I rode up the hill towards my pad for the night. A high-rise motel that looked like it had been closed for at least fifty years, surrounded on all sided by towering, prison-yard fences. An overweight woman with a roll-up cigarette in one hand and a baby in the other staggered down the steps as I unclipped my helmet and walked towards the entrance.

I pushed one of the rusty doors open, and shuffled inside. The receptionist sat crammed behind a miniscule desk, throwing leftovers from his sandwich to the unkempt golden labrador sniffing at his feet. After giving my name, this young man explained that he needed to go and check if the room I had booked was free and clean. Earlier that morning, I had reserved a room on the ground floor in order to make life easier with the bike. My friend quickly returned and explained that the only available room was on the third floor. I wasn't in the mood to fight.

After a few fragmented hours of sleep in the world's squeakiest bunk bed, I pulled on my Northern Ireland shirt and threw my bike over my shoulder to edge perilously down the motel's spiral staircase.

"Is there a breakfast?" I asked the receptionist from the previous night.

"Pardon?"

"Breakfast? Petit déjeuner? It said on your website you provided it."

"Ahhh petit déjeuner!" he replied with a look of mild panic on his face, whilst scavenging around his desk for whatever morsels he could find.

He gathered together a small plastic carton of orange juice and a cereal bar. I suppose it was better than nothing. In a way, I respected how little effort he put into running his business. There was a raw honesty about him that it was hard not to admire.

I waved goodbye, dodging his rabid dog as I left, and it didn't take long for the rain to arrive. Starting as a comforting trickle, it soon developed into a torrential downpour. Every couple of minutes, another bucketful of lying water was thrown into my face by a passing van or lorry. I hid under a tree for half an hour in Melun, hoping upon hope that it would ease. I devoured an entire loaf of soggy brioche while I waited. And waited. No change was forthcoming, so I slid back onto my wet saddle and puffed and panted past lines of disbelieving drivers in traffic jams once again.

The rain was incessant. Like nothing I've ever known before. Water streamed off the visor on my helmet like a portable Niagara Falls. Any moisture not falling from the sky was sprayed back up towards my face from the vast puddles I sloshed through. And it was freezing. This wasn't soothing, tropical rain. It was like being trapped in a cold shower for seven hours.

My hands started to visibly shake in front of me. Trembling as I grasped the handles with my bluish-white fingers, I could just make out an industrial estate through the mist less than half a mile away. This was tough. Really tough. And there was still another one or two hours to go, from what I could see. I was now so cold and wet that it had become difficult to think straight, let alone pedal straight. Stopping outside a McDonalds in an unknown, uninspiring suburb of Paris, I fumbled as I turned the key in my bike lock and quickly clasped my pannier bags in a heap in my arms.

I've had baths less wet than that final cycle into Paris

I ran into the warm embrace of the disabled toilets, and immediately stripped naked. Every last scrap came off. Shivering head to toe from the battering I'd received all day from the elements, I held each item of clothing under the hand-drier and spared a thought for the fine, upstanding people who had opened this particular branch of McDonalds not knowing that it might one day save a young man's life.

I slumped to the floor. Sitting with my back to the wall and my bum cheeks to the tiled floor, I allowed the warm gust of air from the hand-dryer to blow through my sodden head of hair. Every thirty seconds I would reach my right hand above my head and restart the flow of air, my eyes fixed on the wall directly ahead of me. A series of loud knocks began to rattle the door, and an impatient French mother cried out despairingly over the noise of her wailing child. It took me a minute or two before I even cared if I was stopping other locals from using the facilities. I clambered to my feet, threw my cycling gear back on, and made my way back to the dining area.

In the end, the hand-dryer hadn't dried anything. It seemed like a bright idea at the time, but it just left the clothes warm and wet instead of cold and wet. It's hard to say which was worse. As I clutched my second cup of coffee in quick succession, I sat on a high stool and gazed out the window at Finn in his sorry, soggy state locked to a bin.

The rain wasn't easing, my legs were completely knackered, and I didn't have the first clue how to ride a pushbike into one of the busiest cities in the world. Parisian drivers are notoriously impatient, and use their car horn more often than the average person breathes out. I was anxious, I was fed up, and I was frozen. I wiped a blanket of moisture from my phone screen and started searching online for taxis to take me the last stretch of my journey into the city. Only fifteen miles from the finish line, and I had finally resorted to making plans for how to give up.

Solihull in the West Midlands has produced an impressive roll call of the great and the good over the years, with Karren Brady off the Apprentice and Top Gear's Richard Hammond amongst its most famous exports. But one name stands head and shoulders above the rest.

On 3rd July 1991, while I was getting swept up in the excitement surrounding my upcoming third birthday, a footballing giant called William Donald Grigg was born.

We've had some fantastic granny-rulers over the years. By this I mean players who may never have set foot in Northern Ireland, but qualify to pull on the green and white shirt due to Article 1(c) in the criteria for eligibility to represent a home nation – that "one of his (the player's) biological grandparents was born on the territory of the relevant Association." From our current crop alone, we have a huge amount to thank the grandparents of Ollie Norwood, Jamie Ward and Conor Washington for.

Player eligibility is without doubt the prickliest of prickly points when chatting about the Northern Ireland football team. In terms of the politics of 'identity', there are very few places on Earth like here. All natives of our unique country are eligible for dual nationality, and can therefore carry both British and Irish passports at the same time. So, if you're a footballer from Belfast – for example – and feel more Irish than you do Northern Irish or British, you can choose to play for the Republic of Ireland. Even if you've already represented Northern Ireland at junior level. The fact that this same rule does not apply to enable players from down south to come and play for Northern Ireland often leaves us feeling like the victims of one-way robbery.

However, despite the players we lose to emigration south of the border, we continue to gain the occasional gem of a footballer from across the water. Young men looking to make their grannies proud. Which brings me back to Will Grigg.

In the months leading up to Euro 2016 he was slamming goals in on a regular basis for his club, Wigan Athletic, and a chant emerged amongst their fans to the tune of mid-nineties dancefloor anthem "*Freed from Desire*". Whether or not defenders have ever really been terrified, the song gained momentum online and quickly became a YouTube sensation.

If you haven't heard it before (and you *really* must have been hiding under a very large rock if that's the case), here's how it goes:

> *Will Grigg's on fire, your defence is terrified (x3)*
>
> *Will Grigg's on fire… OOOH!*
>
> *Na na na na na na na na na na na na….*

Belting out the 'OOOH!' – that one lung-emptying burst of sound – while throwing a fist high in the air with 20,000 other Northern Ireland fanatics is one of the most euphoric feelings I've experienced inside a football stadium. Followed by endless bouncing and hugging and prancing around like the weight of every care in the world has temporarily been lifted from your shoulders.

As it turned out, Will Grigg never made it on to the pitch at Euro 2016. From our squad of twenty-three, he and two other outfield players unfortunately experienced the disappointment of not featuring in any of our matches. But in a strange, skewed way, this made him even more of a hero in our eyes. It made us want to shout louder and longer. Besides, a large part of the fun of singing his name for fifteen minutes uninterrupted was to see him shuffling awkwardly on the subs bench pretending that he couldn't hear us. It would only have been a distraction for him if he'd been on the pitch.

Glancing into my wallet, I promptly noted that I had no Euros left. Not even one. The only thing now funding my ever-worsening McDonalds addiction was my old, faithful Ulster Bank debit card. And I knew that wasn't going to be much use when haggling with an impatient Parisian cabbie.

Hailstones pelted the window immediately in front of where I sat. I shivered just thinking about stepping into that deluge again. Just then, my phone buzzed. It was a new message from the WhatsApp group I have with Jonny and Wes – called 'Michael O'Neill's a Legend' (an ironic name created by Wes to annoy me during Michael's first year in office when – I'm ashamed to admit – I was an aggressively vocal critic of our gaffer).

"Where have you got to?" asked Wes.

"Somewhere near Paris. This weather is insane," I replied, emphasising my alarm using the monkey-with-hands-over-his-eyes emoji.

"Don't meet us at the Eiffel Tower like you said you would Stevo, that's miles from our place. Come find us at the zoo. We're taking the subway over there now."

And just like that, it was decided. After a shade over 2100 miles of cycling, Wes and Jonny had made the call that I would roll across my finish line at one of the most iconic landmarks in Paris. Not the Eiffel Tower. Not the Arc de Triomphe. Not Notre Dame.

No, the zoo.

Since going our separate ways in Lyon, those two had spent the past four days swanning about on their own romantic package holiday. They'd even taken in another match in sunny Saint Etienne with the spare time they had on their hands – coincidentally the one between Czech Republic and Croatia where the atmosphere turned a tad feisty, with supporters chucking fireworks and ripped-up chairs at one another. It amazes me how Eastern European fans always manage to sneak flares into football stadiums, but I get turned away if I try and carry in a plastic bottle of Coke with its lid still on.

Before I could meet my two globetrotting companions, I had to somehow muster the motivation to not only get back on my bike but first step out the door and into the raging storm. With images now swirling around my mind of Jonny flicking crumbs of crusty bread to tropical birds and Wes being chased around the meerkat enclosure, I grimaced in the face of the torrential downpour and climbed aboard my saddle with renewed optimism, squelching as I plonked my rear end on to the saddle once more.

The following hour was like something lifted out of a sketch show. Either that or a Shakespearean tragedy. Every ten minutes the rain grew stronger and harder and heavier than it had been before. Just when you thought it couldn't get any more severe, it did. If I had turned around to see the Gendarme firing water cannons at me from either side of the road, it honestly wouldn't have taken me by surprise.

I had reached the point where I didn't even feel wet anymore. Wet had become the new normal. Hailstones sprung off the back of my fluorescent yellow coat, making a noise of strikingly percussive quality over the background din of lorries and cars careering through puddles several inches deep on the dual carriageway.

Having ridden with my head down and eyes half-closed for most of the final approach into the outer reaches of Paris city centre, I lifted my gaze and noticed a body of water flowing past at an impressive rate of knots across from the traffic lights where I had stopped. The name of this suburb, Vitry-sur-Seine, quickly gave away the name of the river that I'd discovered. Finally, the home stretch.

I wasn't familiar with much Parisian geography, but I did know that the River Seine sliced through the middle of the city like a knife and by following its banks from this point on I was unlikely to go very far wrong. Pushing on through Ivry-sur-Seine and into the 13th arrondissement, I swung across one of Paris's thirty-seven bridges and aimed for the zoo.

As if to welcome me into its warm arms, the rain relented as I arrived in Paris. I couldn't find any roadsigns for the zoo, and so I staggered across to a police van that was parked outside a tall block of flats.

"Bonjour monsieur! Bonjour!" I yelled, knocking firmly on the window of his van to grab his attention.

He wound down his window at an unnervingly slow speed, and stared back at me. Like he was staring deep into my soul. Those kind of eyes.

"Je voudrais aller à la Parc Zoologique," I spluttered. "Où est la Parc Zoologique?"

Still without uttering a word, he lifted his arm to take a look at his watch. As he checked the time, I saw the gun strapped to his belt and my heart rate started to tick along that little bit faster.

His head rolled back towards me, and he took a deep breath in.

"La parc zoologique est fermé."

Yes, I know it's closed you numbskull. I just want to meet Jonny and Wes at the entrance. I had no idea how to tell him that in French though.

"Mais où est la parc zoologique?" I repeated, like Jeremy Paxman on his summer holidays. I may not be fluent but I'm persistent.

He reached for the door handle, flung it wide open and stepped outside. I couldn't tell exactly how tall he was, but this guy was missing a trick by not playing basketball for a living. Towering over me to such an extent that his gun was now dancing dangerously close to my face, he pointed one of his colossal arms ahead of him and barked at me to take the third road on the right – "la troisième route à droite".

I thanked him for his kindness and clear directions, and didn't get even the slightest flicker of a smile in return. He didn't trust me one bit. The look of suspicion was painted all over his face. He'd obviously seen my type loitering around the zoo before. I fully expect that he crawled along a few hundred metres behind me as I sped off, convinced that he was on the cusp of the greatest scoop of his policing career. Waiting like a predator to catch me red-handed on my late night penguin-stealing mission.

The shadow from the high-rise apartment block soon vanished, and I was instead surrounded by large canopies of trees overhead. The frenzied noise of parrots and monkeys soared through the air, and I veered left at a sign pointing me towards the main entrance of the zoo.

I freewheeled under a black canvas banner saying 'PARC ZOOLOGIQUE DE PARIS' in capital letters, as Jonny's inimitable voice rang out from only a few metres away.

"Yeeeoooooo! Nice summer's day for a bike ride, Stevo."

"How's the derrière?" chimed Wes, gorging on a packet of Wine Gums.

"Tender," I replied. "So good to see you lads. And so *unbelievably* glad I'm done."

Mission accomplished

Then, in one of the most tragic anti-climaxes of my life so far, Jonny insisted on getting me to go back round the corner with my bike, and (slowly) pedal back through the mud-soaked finish line once more, as he'd forgotten to press the 'Record' button on his phone the first time around.

"Nice and dry there?" chuckled Wes, his voice muffled beneath a mountain of t-shirts, coats and scarves.

"Here, hold this," I said, pushing my bike in his direction. I'd only stopped moving, but I was already starting to shiver. I reached deep into my rear left pannier bag and grabbed the first reasonably dry top I could lay my hands on. I stripped off my top half outside the entrance to the zoo, and we hastily shuffled towards the metro together.

"Let's get you back to our palace then, Stevo," suggested Jonny, his voice thick with poorly-veiled sarcasm.

"Can't wait for a lie down," I said. "Is it decent?"

Jonny put one hand on my shoulder, looked me square in the eyes and replied with a devious smile.

"You're in for a treat."

A beam of sunlight penetrated through the flimsy beige curtains, and I rolled over in bed to scratch the intense itch on my left arm. They had been back again. My arm suddenly had the bearings of an amputation-worthy skin condition, with ten or fifteen angry red craters growling up at me.

I accept we weren't paying top-end prices to stay at the Bastille Hostel, located in a back-alley to the east of the city centre, but still we didn't expect to be eaten alive by bedbugs. No matter which room they sent us to, there always seemed to be an army of skin-devouring parasites waiting for darkness to fall to do their dirty deed.

And yes, you read that correctly. Sent to different rooms. Not just on the odd occasion, but every single night. I hadn't been submitting complaints asking to move (though I often wonder whether I should have), but rather it was down to the hostel staff's obsession with making life as difficult as possible for their guests. Maybe they just didn't like the look of the three of us. We will never know.

The staff roped in by that bustling hostel were rude beyond belief. I reckon it was probably part of the job description. The whole place was ramshackle and chaotic, from its creaking prison beds and treacherous, cracked wooden staircase to the flies landing on croissants at the breakfast table, and so the Fawlty Towers-esque staff were simply the icing on the cake. The only issue was we couldn't exactly argue, since we were paying peanuts to stay there.

Paris can be very expensive – on wide boulevards closer to the centre, you can stay in picturesque apartments that you'd need to sell your wife and kids for, or wander wide-eyed at the sight of supercars and obscenely overpriced handbags in shop windows. Give me a Ford Fiesta and Tesco Bag for Life any day of the week. And since we weren't doling out the kind of Euros that ensure you come away from your bed with bite-free arms, I resigned to the fact that for however long I remained in the capital this would be my small, itchy cross to bear.

Sprinting at full tilt through throngs of supporters marching the other way, I found myself bombarded with hearty cries of "Go on ye boy ye!" and "Run Forrest Run!" I couldn't allow myself to slow down. If I was to have any chance of getting into the Parc des Princes before kick-off, galloping like a man possessed was my only option.

The only ticket I had missed in the ballot earlier in the year was for this final group match against Germany. It was always going to be the most popular match if our fans had to choose only one – taking on the flair, skill and dynamism of the world champions right in the heart of Paris, and with it so easily accessible from the array of low-cost travel into its two airports.

Wes and Jonny had secured tickets of their own in the upper tier, while I'd only been put in touch at the last minute with a friend of a friend trying to shift a spare ticket thanks to my dad. Had to somehow find that friend of a friend in the middle of Paris now though.

"Sorry!" I shouted as I knocked a burly German's pint out of his hands.

I would have stopped and bought him another one, but I didn't have the time.

Darting around another corner, I looked at the time on my phone again. 5:50pm. The game was kicking off in ten minutes. I was used to arriving during the first few minutes of matches back in Belfast, but this was different. If I didn't find this person – someone I'd never met or even seen a picture of before – my hopes of witnessing the most crucial football match in a generation would evaporate instantly.

The last dregs of battery had drained from my phone, and the screen finally turned black. I was scuppered. Lost and alone in a crowd of thousands.

All I could do was run.

I paused for a moment on reaching the end of the street, my heart pounding through my chest as I turned my head to the left and right looking for an adult male in a Northern Ireland shirt. Which narrowed it down to around 5,000 people or so. Great.

The reason I'd gone on such a wild goose chase was as a result of the metro station at Porte de Saint-Cloud having two exits. Two exits on completely different roads, with about one mile separating them. Making arranging to meet someone at the exit of the station a little trickier than first expected.

I began to notice gaps in the sea of green and white. The streets were emptying. Without announcement a mass migration moved in the direction of the stadium, and I still didn't have a ticket. Two thousand and one hundred miles suddenly felt like a very long way to travel to be refused entry at the turnstiles.

A thud hit me in the middle of my back, nearly knocking me to the ground.

"Stephen? Is it Stephen?" came the anguished voice.

"Yes, are you…I mean, have you got the…?"

"Tickets? Aye, let's go! We need to get a move on, mate."

We barged our way through the boisterous crowd at the gates, and bounded up the steps into the cavernous Parc des Princes. The introduction to the German national anthem crackled over the loud speakers. And their fans were up for it. Up to that point in the tournament, the only real disappointment I could think of had been the lack of vocal presence amongst the opposing fans at our games. That was about to change.

The picture most of us have in our heads of the typical German being serious, uptight and about as much fun as a kick in the groin couldn't be further from the truth. At least not based on their football fans. Not only did they continually bounce off our supporters with their own raucous chants, but they *joined in* with ours. One united choir soon assembled of almost 50,000 voices, singing "*Will* (or Vill to those in the German end) *Grigg's on Fire*". It was just as ironic coming from their set of fans as it was from ours, with poor Will not playing for either team during his month in France.

Half way up the Eiffel Tower with ze Germans on the morning of matchday

The game was a carnival from start to finish. I've never experienced an atmosphere like it, taking into account each and every single supporter in the ground. There was no malice, but just loud – very loud – celebration everywhere you looked. And we all had reason to celebrate. Germany had secured their place in the knock-out stages, and we knew that as long as we didn't get massacred we would probably also qualify as one of best third-placed teams thanks to the momentous victory in our previous match.

There were memories to be made here first though. Just shy of thirty years after the Germans had torn down a fairly impressive

177

wall of their own, we were intent on building a new one for them. A wall that started at one of our goalposts and reached across to the other. Consisting of one man.

Yes, one of their uglier attempts bobbled over the line, but for the rest of the match Michael McGovern was supreme. Our very own Secretary of Defence. Götze tried, Müller tried, Özil tried, but no matter how many maestros with two dots over a random letter in their name had a go, they couldn't add to the tally. Twenty-eight shots peppered our goal, and only one squeaked through. Germany could have been out of sight by half-time if it wasn't for Magic Mike and his omnipresent outstretched arms and legs.

Every time you thought things had reached fever pitch, a sporadic event on or off the pitch would cause the volume to ratchet up another notch. The dancing was only suspended for half a minute towards the end of the first half when Kyle Lafferty's supermodel wife was spotted by an eagle-eyed spectator near us and the whole stand serenaded her until she acknowledged her 10,000 suitors with a bashful wave.

By the mid-point of the second half, my thighs were aching from the repetitive squatting action of bouncing up and down on the spot. Yes, I'd cycled a few miles to get here, but this GAWA-orchestrated aerobic workout was pounding the poor muscles in my legs more than any 100-miler on the roads. I eventually stood still and allowed myself a moment mid-song to catch my breath. And what I felt is something I will never forget. The earth was shaking.

Tremors pulsated through the stand. With every collective leap from the Northern Irish faithful, the ground actually moved beneath my feet. My body shook like a fat man holding a pneumatic drill. Suddenly, the game being abandoned due to the stadium collapsing was becoming a distinct possibility. Would it be declared a draw if that was to happen? Hold on, maybe there's a Plan B we could go for in the last ten minutes, I thought to myself.

We lost the match by one Mario Gomez goal to nil but barely heard the final whistle, lost as we were to the world in the jubilant scenes unfolding in the stands. I wasn't too sure about the exact helping hands we needed in order to qualify as a best third-placed team, but big Wes had it sussed. Having worked in accounts for years, he was all over the number crunching.

"So, if Turkey win tonight," he explained as we filed into the pavilion area outside the stadium, sweaty bodies pressing against us on all sides, "we're through."

"That's definitely all we need?" asked Jonny.

"Yep, that'd do it."

"Turkey, fair enough," I nodded. "Suppose I don't dislike them too much to be a fan for a night."

"Wait...hold on fellas! Look!" We turned around and saw Jonny frozen in time three paces behind us. "Look, it's Brunty!"

One of our longest-serving players, Chris Brunt, had the misfortune of picking up an anterior cruciate ligament injury just a month earlier playing for his club side, West Bromwich Albion. Having dreamt of pulling on the green and white jersey at a major championship since his boyhood days in South Belfast, it was a devastating blow. For us, he has often remained quiet for large chunks of matches over the years, only to turn up out of nowhere and flip a game on its head with a meticulous corner or free-kick. The sort of pinpoint deliveries, to be honest, we were missing badly in France.

"Chris, Chris!" I shrieked, almost tripping as I ran up to him. "What did you make of that?"

"Amazing, wasn't it?" added Jonny.

"Aye, s'pose so." His body language was a world apart from the lively buzz of Northern Ireland fans around him. "Yeah. I don't know, I found it pretty hard to watch."

Bruntosaurus Rex, outside the Parc des Princes

You could tell it still hurt. Not the pain in his knee, but the pain of missing moments like that afternoon, the like of which may never come round again for him. He graciously posed for a souvenir photo with the lads, his face as glum as a dyslexic in a library. We wished him well, and told him he was welcome round the Bastille Hostel any time.

Later that evening we became honorary Turks and celebrated long into the night with boisterous revellers, as cinema screens at the foot of the Eiffel Tower projected images of Turkey's thrilling win over the Czech Republic. I say thrilling, it might not have been. But it definitely felt that way for those of us with our future in the competition depending on the outcome. When full time came, fezzes flew through the air and we were swept into a scrum of dancing, bearded Middle Eastern men.

The great irony was that Turkey themselves didn't even qualify for the next round after disappointing defeats in their previous two matches. Elimination for them could not be avoided thanks to the cruel footballing curse of inferior goal difference. They might not have done what they needed, but they had done what *we* needed.

And if that mob of sweaty, overweight friends are the only Turkish people I ever meet (outside a late-night kebab shop context), that will be enough for me. Thanks to their team's gutsy last-ditch endeavours, Finn and I weren't going home yet.

Just before leaving the hostel to join Wes and Jonny for one final meal out before they traipsed back to their lonely wives and nine-to-fives, I took it upon myself to sort out further accommodation while I still remembered.

"Hi, I'd like to book a room for the next two nights please. Is that possible?"

The work experience girl behind the till looked at me over her thin-rimmed red glasses, displaying an expression of utter disgust that I would have the audacity to even ask her such a question. She was learning fast from her future employers.

"We are very busy."

Glancing around the deserted foyer and lounge area, with only a grainy miniature TV in the corner playing old Eurovision classics, I found this difficult to believe.

"Is it possible you could check if there's space?" I asked.

She glared at me for a good five seconds, then spun around in her swivel chair and angrily punched a handful of buttons on her keyboard.

"Yes, zere is a single room. On ze fifth floor."

Not ideal, with me currently staying on the second floor and having to cart all my belongings up that perilous spiral staircase once more, but I suppose needs must.

"Fair enough, can I pay now?"

"You can pay for tonight *only*," she snapped. "Zen we will move you."

"Why?"

"Zat room is booked by someone else for tomorrow night."

I stared her in the eyes to see if she was being serious. I didn't want to insult the perishingly small amount of intelligence that she appeared to possess, but surely even she could see through her flawed logic. So I gave her a helping hand.

"And can you not move the *other people?*"

"Which people?" she replied, confused.

"The ones who are coming tomorrow night? And keep me in the same room?"

"Non. Zey have booked your room for tomorrow. You must move to anozer room before zen."

"Will I be moving to a single room tomorrow?"

"Yes. A different single room."

"So you *could* put the other person in that different single room?"

"Non. Zat is impossible, because zey have booked your room."

I could have spent all evening drawing diagrams to illustrate my point, but I'd have been wasting my time. It was like trying to explain rocket science to a fish.

Abandoning this pointless exercise, I staggered up the staircase to my new temporary pad on the fifth floor. As I fumbled around in my pocket trying to find the key, I wondered if maybe that girl at reception was trying to reach out with a generous offer. Maybe I shouldn't have been so condescending.

Perhaps this room was the finest bedroom in the entire hostel – even the whole of Paris – and other guests couldn't just be expected to forego staying in it. What if I opened this door, and saw a four-poster bed with a fresh pain au chocolat perched on the pillow? What if there was a balcony looking out over uninterrupted views of cool water gushing along the Seine, while portrait painters flicked smiles up at me from underneath their berets? What if she had done me an incredibly good turn by allowing me a night in such majestic surroundings?

The lock clicked as I turned the key, and I slowly edged the door open.

Where the four-poster bed should have stood was a sweat-stained sheet on a single bed that sank ominously in the middle. Where I'd imagined the leaf-lined balcony was a small rusty window that refused to shut, opening permanently out onto the racket of traffic and car horns on the street below. Cracked tiles lay scattered across the floor beneath my feet, and a sub-human stench was emanating from the bathroom.

Letting out a sigh, I chucked my pannier bags in a heap on the bed, switched off the flickering light bulb, and clambered down the staircase to rejoin the boys at the front door.

As Wes and Jonny hot-footed it on to the Métro for the airport, I slinked towards the city centre. Although it was now guaranteed that Northern Ireland had qualified for the next round, it was far from set in stone who we would stride into battle with. And as such, I had no idea where my travels would take me next. If anywhere, that is.

I wouldn't know until the following night.

With the tournament organisers using a ranking system so complicated it would have left Pythagoras scratching his head, several hours of number-crunching were needed to establish that our next contest would either be an almighty clash against the host nation France in Lyon, or a passionate, nail-your-colours-to-the-mast Celtic duel with Wales back at the Parc des Princes.

This left a fifty percent chance that I would not have to cycle a centimetre further.

My heart and mind were ready to get back to business in the service of my country if called upon, but I knew deep down that a holiday from cycling wouldn't exactly be a kick in the teeth. My more intimate regions were only beginning to regain sensation, and the cushioned stools of the Parisian cafés I was frequenting had become considerably more appealing than any bike seat you could push in my direction.

And who was to decide my fate? That responsibility fell into the hands of the most unlikely band of volunteers. The boys in green from the other side of the border. The Republic of Ireland. The one team that many of us still can't properly decide what to think of.

Their federation poach a decent number of our young players – they've even nabbed their manager from north of the border – and they infuriatingly love to claim they're the only team in Ireland. Having said all that, their fans are incredibly inventive when it comes to fancy dress and they love a good sing-song, so we can allow a certain degree of leeway. And more importantly at this moment in time, they held the key to me staying put for a further four days in the capital.

Clambering up the rain-soaked steps from the darkness of the metro station that evening and ordering an extortionately expensive beer at a roadside café, I sat with a small crowd of locals in front of a TV screen to embark on the previously unthinkable. Cheering on the boys from the South.

Ten minutes remained on the clock. Neither side looked like scoring.

"What time d'ya reckon you'll have to leave in the morning?" asked Nellie, having joined me to watch the tail end of the game.

"Was just thinking that myself."

"How far are we talking?"

"Three hundred miles," I said, with a poorly disguised sigh. "And three days to do it."

It was the mental aspect of what was in store that concerned me. Trudging in reverse along the same roads from only a few days before. The same trees to look at, the same rivers to cross, the same hills to scale. Only backwards. A large part of what had spurred me on up to that point was the intrigue of looking forward to something new and exciting on the landscape each morning.

"Does it not kill to sit on a bike seat for that long every day?" said Nellie.

I nodded and took another sip from my pint glass.

"But after a couple of hours everything goes numb down below, and then it's not just as bad."

Suddenly, the table next to us leapt to their feet and the remainder of my drink was thrown over my lap. On the screen high in the corner of the outside terrace, white-shirted Irish players skidded on their knees across the turf in celebration.

"Did they just score?" I asked loudly, to anyone able to respond.

"Oui! C'est un but pour Irlande!" yelled a well-boozed Frenchman leaping from the café windowsill, hopping from one foot to the other without spilling a drop of his red wine.

Nellie looked and me and asked, "Does this mean you're not...?"

"Yeah!" I gasped. "If it stays this way, I'm going nowhere!"

When the final whistle blew five minutes later, I leapt to my feet and hugged Nellie like I'd just won the Euromillions.

In an act of tremendous cross-border generosity, Robbie Brady had stuck his head on a hopeful punt forward and in doing so had saved me from days of pain. Quite literally. I had never been so thrilled to see the Republic of Ireland win a game of football.

"Gracias Robbie Brady!" I yelled. "Or whatever 'Thank you' is in Irish."

"Is it Wales next then?" said Nellie, his voice echoing as I shook myself out of the daydream I'd drifted into.

"Uh-huh, yeah." My head was on another planet. "I mean, at least I think so."

"What does that mean for you?"

"Five. More. Days." I said, punctuating each word to get the message across loud and clear. "No cycling for five more days!"

The following morning, I took an extra half an hour eating breakfast. Everything felt lazy and carefree. It was bliss. I spent the morning milling around the Arc de Triomphe, where I was seized by a local journalist who had spotted my green and white jersey and was looking for insight from a UK native on the previous day's shock results in the Brexit referendum. The interview was conducted in French, and I just about got by with my very small collection of words.

"Did you vote?" he asked, holding his dictaphone close to my chin.

"No."

"Why not?"

"Because I've been in France."

"Are you upset?"

I thought for a brief moment before shaking my head and saying, "No."

"Why not?"

"Because Northern Ireland are still in the Euros."

He looked stunned by my lack of engagement with this colossal story. You could see it in his eyes. This is world-changing news, he was thinking. Why doesn't this Northern Irish oddball seem to care? He was determined to get a soundbite.

"Do you think people will start fighting again in Ireland because of the Brexit vote?" he continued.

"No"

"Why not?"

"Because both our teams are still in the Euros"

"Do you have any other concerns?" he said, firing one final, hopeful question at me.

"Yes," I replied. "Gareth Bale."

It was half past eleven before we found a table. The aroma of meticulously-grilled steak hung in the air as we stepped in from the cobbled streets and took our perch in the midst of the raucous cafe. Benjamin – a former uni housemate of mine, born and raised in Paris – had invited me to join him and some pals for a traditional French feast. Congregating around a grubby picnic table that was the only available seat in the house, a waiter appeared and scrubbed the wooden surface with his cloth before sauntering off again in the direction of the bar.

My unexpected Parisian holiday had flown by in an absolute blur. After three weeks of nothing but pedal stroke after pedal stroke, I was determined to pack as much into these bonus days as possible. One morning was spent in the sun-soaked back alleys of Montmartre having breakfast with other Northern Ireland fans while a street artist frantically sketched my portrait. I did a training run up the Eiffel Tower late one evening, skipping up two steel steps at a time as floodlit elevators darted up and down on cables around me. I was even accosted by the police in the early hours of one morning as I returned back to my hostel after a night out.

"Hey, you!" shouted the muscular, unshaven officer from the passenger seat of his van.

"Yes?" I replied hesitantly, nearly dropping the Happy Meal in my hands with the fright.

"Are you from Irlande du Nord?"

"Yes."

The five armoured policemen inside the van looked at one another, and after a few seconds the driver gave a knowing nod to his colleagues. I craned my neck round to see one of the officers in the back seat flash a worrying grin.

In unison they looked back in my direction, and after a countdown by the chief officer in the front seat that felt like a lifetime, they started singing.

"Will Grigg's on fiiiiiirrreeee, OOOOOH! Na na na na na na na, na na na, na na!"

The two officers in the front of the van reached from behind their bullet-proof window and shook my hand heartily. As I staggered away into the night, shaking my head and smiling, I turned around as I crossed the road at the traffic lights, only to see a small riot van in the distance bobbing side to side with dancing and the sound of hysterical laughter ringing through the air.

Hugo threw the menus to one side before anyone else had a chance to take a look.

"Zere is only one zing we are aving tonight" he screamed, hammering both fists on the table to add a sense of urgency to his words.

"Is it snails?" I asked.

"Non, even more French zan zat."

"Frog legs?"

"Nobody eats frog legs. Well, may-bay some strange parts of ze countryside. But not in Paree."

I was rapidly running out of ideas. "Baguettes? Onions? Cheese?"

"Non, Stephen" – or Steve-hen as he insisted on pronouncing it – "tonight wiz us you will ave... MOULE FRITES!"

As soon as he uttered the words, the other three cheered at the top of their voices and stamped their feet like a pack of builders who had just stumbled upon Miss Universe.

"You must ave moules or you will never be a proper Frenchman!"

They hadn't even had much to drink up to that point. One glass of wine before leaving their flat earlier, maybe two. But the thought of a plate of patriotic cuisine had rendered the lot of them intoxicated with blue, white and red coursing through their veins. I was half expecting the West End cast of *Les Mis* to burst through the door belting out a few numbers, just to add to the nationalistic sense of occasion.

We made our order, and before long what looked like four large plant pots were placed in front of us.

"They're greasy little fellas, aren't they?" I said, picking another rubbery chunk of mussel from between my teeth.

"A leetle beet. What do you zink of zem?"

I reached into the silver bucket for my next shell.

"Very salty, to be honest, but I could get used to them."

It felt like I had swallowed half the ocean, but I'd eaten worse. The basket of chips, accompanied by a steady supply of mayonnaise, soon disappeared with the four of us gobbling all before us like a lifesize game of Hungry Hungry Hippos.

"Don't ave zat one!" shouted Remi all of a sudden.

"Why, do you want it?"

"Non, eet is still closed."

I quickly tossed the offending uncooked mussel onto the tray at the end of our table. The very last thing I needed was to spend the following day chucking my guts up into a bin at the Parc des Princes instead of watching our last-sixteen clash against the Welsh.

"There's an Irish song about moules, lads." It had reached the time of night where I was feeling educational. "Want me to teach you it?"

The rest of the table nodded their approval excitedly, while I cleared my throat.

For the next half an hour, boisterous and increasingly tuneless renditions of *'Molly Malone'* rang out from that small mussel café on Rue Mouffetard.

The Midnight Mussel-Eating Choir

"But *why* did she have to die?" cried Hugo, genuinely despondent by this stage.

"Because of a fever," I explained.

"And no-one could save her!" sang Benjamin loudly, pounding the table with his fist to highlight the gravity of poor Molly's plight, and also showing off the fact that he'd already memorised all the words.

With Hugo now fighting off tears, and the staff dropping ever more subtle hints about wanting us to leave the empty tavern so they could head home, we grabbed our coats and made tracks for the dimly-lit streets outside.

Clutching tightly to the scrap of damp, slightly torn paper in my grasp, I looked down and unfurled my ticket to slide it into the jaws of the scanner built into the walls of the royal blue turnstile.

The bass drum was already thundering, its noise drawing closer with every step.

"BOOM BOOM (silence)…BOOM BOOM (silence)…"

A pregnant pause between every double beat offered an invitation for anyone with a connection to Northern Ireland to fill in the blanks – "Green and White Arrrmy!"

This was the game nobody had prepared for.

Of all the Euro 2016 holidays arranged in the year leading up to the tournament, only the bravest Northern Ireland fans had factored in the remote possibility that we might still be hanging around after the group stage. Even though we had joked about our path to lifting the trophy with block-booking mates in the terraces, deep down nobody had dared to believe that there might be more.

Company for lunch pre-match had consisted of my mate, Mark, and a Welsh family of five who we'd met at one of the many crammed roadside cafés. Red dragons were scrawled across their cheeks in face paint, and scarves and flags had been fastened to any table, lamp or coatstand that they could lay their hands on.

The atmosphere rumbled for miles around. Wales hadn't qualified for a European championships in their history, making this game arguably even more significant for their fans.

"What do yooooo rehhhhh-ckon the score will beeeee then?" asked David, the blonde-haired eldest son of the Welsh clan, in his lilting accent just as food arrived at our table.

"It's hard to separate the teams," I said. "If it wasn't for Bale, I reckon we'd be favourites."

"Bale's all they need though, boy," added Mark, chewing a mouthful of his steakburger as he spoke.

Calm before the storm - enjoying lunch with a family of Welsh dragons

If you ever needed a dictionary definition of a team carried by one player, Wales and Gareth Bale are that team. With a starting eleven of ten unspectacular grafters and one undeniable genius, they are a troublesome and unpredictable quantity. Bale has moulded himself into one of the very best players in the world since making the bold switch of swapping London for life overseas and playing amidst the cut-throat catwalk of talent at Real Madrid. The Spanish top flight, or *La Liga*, has a notoriously hostile media and footballers who fail to meet their lofty expectations – and there are many unfortunate British examples from recent memory – are chewed up and spat out before they even have time to learn the Spanish for "You're fired."

The fact that Bale flourished in a Madrid side that for years contained Cristiano Ronaldo, arguably the greatest player of his generation, speaks volumes for the natural gifting of the top-knotted wizard from Cardiff. If we were to have any chance whatsoever of overcoming the men in red, there was only one teamtalk that Michael O'Neill needed to dish out. Stick to Bale like a rash. We couldn't give him room to breathe. Mind you, that is easier said than done.

"Anyone want tickeeeeeeeets?" cried a leather-jacket clad man walking past the café where we sat. "Match tickeeeeeeeets?"

Mark and I knew dozens of friends back in Northern Ireland who had been living on Ebay and Seatwave for the past week trying to find any way possible of getting into the ground for this game. Tickets were like gold dust, and Mark didn't have a lot of time for a back-alley entrepreneur looking to make a profit from fans who had travelled from Belfast to Paris via the likes of Italy, Greece and Ibiza (all genuine trips taken by desperate Northern Irish supporters we had met that day) without a match ticket to show between them.

"Why are ya selling them?" shouted Mark.

"Aaah, I bought too many mate," came the reply in a thick Cockney accent.

"So you're going to the game yourself?"

"Yeah, b-b-but just need to shift a few spares," the tout replied, slowly beginning to realise that Mark's interrogation was only going to end one way.

"Which team are you supporting then?"

Mark wasn't letting this one go in a hurry. He was enjoying it too much. It was like watching a young Jack Russell with a chew toy.

"Ehm, yeah, Northern Ireland mate," he said glancing at the shirts on our chests, a look of mild panic now etched across his face.

"Great job, my man. Tell me then, who's your favourite Northern Ireland player?"

The silence that followed was brilliant. The last time I saw a fraud being exposed this impressively, it was on an episode of Panorama. Only difference being that Mark didn't need to knock on doors or hack into any email accounts to make the most of his investigative skills.

"Don't worry, it's hard to narrow it down to one player, isn't it?" Mark chimed, a devious grin spreading across his face as he sipped once again from his beer bottle.

Unsurprisingly Del Boy scampered away and the rest of us at the table finally let out the almighty laugh we'd been fighting to hold in for the previous five minutes.

Taking a handful of short steps into the stand between the goal and the corner flag at the Northern Ireland end of the stadium, I stopped and swivelled where I stood, trying as hard as I could to soak it up. I knew that scenes like this, if today wasn't to pan out as we hoped, might not come around again for a very long time. And every other Northern Irish fan knew it too. The cauldron of noise and colour that enveloped me from all sides was overpowering. This was our day in the sun, and we were determined to make it count.

While the red sea of Welsh supporters at the other end of the ground politely sang their one song – *Don't take me home'* – on repeat like a broken record, our fans dominated the pre-match contest off the pitch with thundering drums, dancing and thousands of deliriously excited fans singing themselves hoarse.

There was half an hour to go until kick-off when I took my spot beside a bloke from County Tyrone who was ten times more pumped up for the game than anyone I'd met all day.

"Yessssssss boss!" he howled, walloping my back with his hand as I squeezed past him in our row. "You ready for this?"

"Never been more ready."

"You travelled far, mucker?"

"Just from Belfast, same as everyone else," I replied, deciding that I'd talked about my cycling escapades enough over the past few weeks. "What about yourself?"

"Flew in via Amsterdam this morning, so I did. Woulda swam across if I had to."

"Was it alright getting time off work then?" I asked.

"Nope," he said, looking across at me, then pausing. "So I quit."

I stopped clapping and stared back at him. "You quit your job?"

"Aye," he quipped without a moment's hesitation. "I can always get a new one. No sweat. Jobs come and go. But this might never happen again."

For the first time since Nice, blinding rays of sunshine illuminated the grassy surface as the two sets of players strode out. Some, like Gareth McAuley, walked boldly with heads high and chests pushed out like their very lives depended on the outcome of this contest. Other less experienced players crept behind slightly more gingerly, clinging onto the six year-old mascot's hand for comfort rather than vice versa. For one day only we were the White and Green army, with our change strip of white tops adorning the players' backs in a shameless marketing exercise to flog a few extra shirts.

The referee's whistle is futile on days like this. Two or three minutes were on the clock before I realised that the players weren't having a knockabout, and had actually started the match. The singing never stopped. Not once. Impassioned strains of *The Ulster boys making all the noise…*' segued into George Best's *'Spirit in the Sky'*, before *'You are my Davis'* rolled effortlessly into the infamous David Healy parody of *'Away in a Manger'*. All the classics were being belted from the rooftops. Even ones we hadn't sung for years. It was like a one-night-only greatest hits show from the fans.

The gloved hands of Wayne Hennessey in the Welsh goal were stung early on with an outswinging left-footed drive from Stuart Dallas at his near post. Jamie Ward was feeling adventurous too, and fizzed a shot from outside the box, again requiring a fingertips save. The waves of pressure from Northern Ireland were relentless. At our end of the ground, we stood transfixed. We'd never seen our boys go at a game like this before. It was there for the taking. Every so often the red shirts for Wales would creep forward with the ball but each time they would squander possession, frustrated into uncharacteristic errors by the imperious, dogged back-line of Evans and McAuley.

It felt like the first period had only been going on for ten minutes when the referee's whistle signalled half-time. Around me Northern Ireland supporters buzzed with excitement. Some phoned back home, pleading with uninterested wives and girlfriends to turn on the telly, explaining that something special was about to happen. The remainder continued prancing around like kangaroos on a bouncy castle. The first half had been one way traffic, a persistent onslaught of white shirts towards the sun-scorched sea of Welsh fans behind their goal. It was difficult not to think ahead to who we might face in the quarter finals once this was done and dusted.

After an hour of action, however, the dragon awoke from his lair.

The one player who had remained deathly silent for the first forty-five minutes sprung into life, and there was very little we could do to stop him. He wasn't even close to top gear, but Gareth Bale's third gear is enough to leave most footballers spitting out his dust. A free-kick early in the second half served as an ominous warning shot, its vicious dip as it evaded the wall leaving Michael McGovern unsighted until the very last second. Northern Ireland still possessed an air of confidence on the ball, driving creative players like Bale deeper and deeper, but the Welsh counter attacks were making us look increasingly vulnerable. As heavy legs began to tire, holes started to appear.

With twenty minutes left Michael O'Neill remained intent on pressing for a winner and played another attacking hand. The stocky, dynamic Conor Washington was brought on to relieve Ward who had run himself into the ground, no doubt having shed ten gallons of sweat from badgering the blasé Welsh midfield. Yes, our boys were tiring, but twenty minutes of punishment would last only that. Twenty minutes. Time for one last throw of the dice.

Despite having over two thirds of the seats in the stadium, the Welsh fans had slumped into a state of funereal silence. The anxiety from their end was palpable. Cinema screens in the corners of the ground beamed live images of glum six year-old children, smudged images of leeks and Welsh dragons fading from their cheeks, becoming ever more fidgety at the thought of being dumped out of the biggest tournament in their history by a team of nobodies from across the Irish Sea. All the while our comparatively meagre cohort of supporters were causing an almighty ruckus with arms aloft, blasting out more noise than Heathrow at rush hour.

Even so, it is amazing how quickly such jubilation can be hacked to the ground.

The newly bleached-blonde Aaron Ramsey slid an innocuous ball wide on the left to Gareth Bale. Our defence stood in regimental formation, pressing high to try and force the error. Then, in a passage of play that felt like both half a second and half an hour at the same time, Bale dropped a shoulder and hooked a devilish first-time cross into the six-yard box. The danger zone.

The Welsh frontman, Hal Robson-Kanu, charged at the ball to apply the simplest of finishing touches. Or at least he would have done had he not been denied the opportunity. Not because the keeper managed to snatch it away before he got there (although thousands of Ulster men and women have since dreamt that was the case). Instead, in the cruellest turn of events, Gareth McAuley's despairing lunge to clear his lines ended up diverting the ball in for an own-goal.

And for a few brief seconds, the dancing stopped.

The one-track wonders in red behind the goal suddenly woke from their slumber, and we attempted to slowly clamber back off the ropes as the Welsh drone rang out again. After ten seconds of post-traumatic stress (and not a moment longer), our faithful drummer, Craig, hammered two pounding beats and we were singing again. But different emotions reverberated in our words. We still wanted it – we so desperately wanted it – but our self-belief had taken a terminal blow.

Michael O'Neill's face was etched with a heartbreaking combination of pain, anguish and pride. We'd seen it happen so many times before, but this sucker-punch hurt more than most. Two of the Kings of Lyon, Magennis and McGinn, were thrown on in desperation more than expectation. The boys in white were out on their feet.

When the inevitable whistle blew, ten thousand Northern Irish fans exhaled in unison. This had been the most incredible year of asking "What if…?", and now it was gone in a flash. Family members who had spent their monthly wage on travelling to the continent for this one game embraced one another, while a handful of others slumped into their seats for the first time all afternoon and sat staring blankly ahead. Moments like this in football make it easier to understand Morgan Freeman's stoic character, Red, in The Shawshank Redemption when he says that "Hope can drive a man insane."

It was important that we put our astonishing achievements into perspective. We'd exceeded all expectations, silenced critics, and had come within a whisker of the quarter finals of the biggest prize in European football. As poor McAuley left the pitch with the look of a broken man, we roared a deafening encore until our heroes returned to the playing field once more to receive their plaudits.

When they re-emerged, they stood as a squad for at least half an hour – long after the final Welsh fan had scampered through the exits – applauding our support from behind the corner flag of the largely empty stadium where each adoring Northern Irish fan remained to a man. The players stood deathly still, and did their best to drink in what was around them. Thousands of ordinary people whose dreams *had* come true. If the squad needed reassurance that their efforts hadn't been in vain, they need only have looked around. A handful of them climbed over advertising hoardings to throw mud-stained shirts to fans in the first few rows. Kyle Lafferty nearly ended up completely naked, dishing out his boots, shinpads and shorts as well.

Much, much later we were ushered out by stewards who had been working overtime as a result of our impromptu thanksgiving ceremony. A member of the media approached me on my way to the gates, and asked about my overriding emotion. I explained, without hesitation, that simply being in France in the first place had been like winning the tournament for us. As I shared my final thoughts with this interviewer, a half-cut Welsh fan in a comedy hat jumped on my back.

"I just wanna say one thing," he shouted, putting an arm around my shoulders as he looked down the camera lens. "These fans from Northern Ireland are the greatest fans in the world."

The invites for drinks from Welsh fans continued as we filed back out on to the familiar streets around the Parc des Princes. I finally accept one of their offers, and beckon the two lads I'd been sitting with to come and join us. They agree with little persuasion required, and we wait for the traffic to pass before jogging to the other side of the road.

Before we reach the door of the pub outside the Metro stop at Porte de Saint-Cloud, the high-rise buildings around me become a blur, the chanting falls silent and I'm suddenly back in Belfast before I even know what's going on.

That's where the story always ends these days.

I shake my head with a smile, and realise that I've drifted away again half way through the daily rounds on the ward. It's half past eight in the morning and the rain drums angrily against the windows high on the sixth floor of the Royal Victoria Hospital. Over two years have passed since that hazy afternoon outside the Parc des Princes. I press my stethoscope against the chest of the elderly man lying in front of me and ask him to breathe deeply. The crackles from his infected right lung intersperse themselves with the noise from the constant pounding of the rain outside.

As I walk towards the window to prescribe antibiotics for the gentleman now spluttering behind me, I notice something in the distance. Through thick layers of moisture on the window panes, the imposing white stands of Windsor Park stand above South Belfast. It's late July 2018 and France have just been crowned world champions, at a World Cup tournament that our team missed out on in the most agonising fashion, following another sensational qualifying campaign masterminded by Michael – the unflappable genius fast becoming the greatest thing ever to happen to football in our province.

Only a cruel, incorrect refereeing decision saw us succumb to Switzerland in a two-legged play-off last November and prevented us from planning summer holidays to Russia this year. It might not have been physically possible in my two weeks of annual leave from work, but Moscow is only 2000 miles away (which no longer seems quite so far) and I had made tentative sketches of the route. Suppose I'll have to lay those plans to rest for another time.

But positives dramatically outweigh the negatives for fans of 'Our Wee Country' these days. I remember when simply seeing a goal would have sent the local sports press into meltdown, but our dreams have grown loftier since then. It's amazing how a small amount of on-pitch success involving twenty-three ordinary lads can transform a country. Football isn't a meaningless endeavour that exists just to give people something to moan to their mates about. It fosters a genuine, vibrant sense of community and it inspires people. It helps us believe we can be better. To dare to dream.

Looking up at the clock, I see that I'm slightly behind on my ward round. I unfold the crumpled handover sheet from my pocket, and make my way to the next bed on my list. A grey-haired lady looks up at me, having been admitted with a broken hip after a fall at home. I smile back at her as I scan the patient notes at the foot of her bed.

Her name is Caroline.

Route Map across France

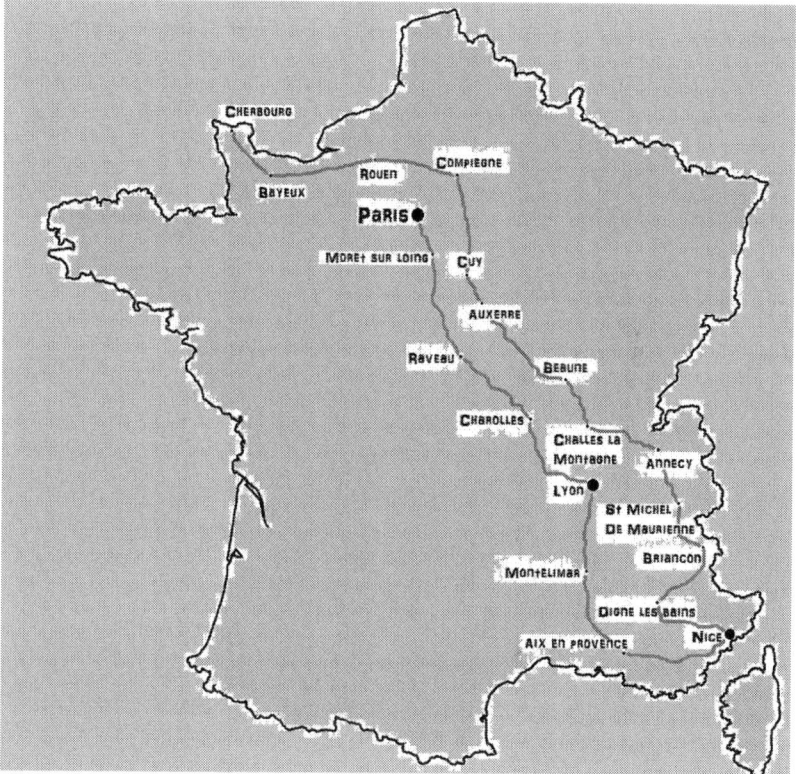

CHERBOURG

COMPIEGNE

ROUEN

BAYEUX

PARIS●

MORET SUR LOING GUY

AUXERRE

RAVEAU BEAUNE

CHAROLLES

CHALLES LA MONTAGNE ANNECY

LYON●

St MICHEL DE MAURIENNE

BRIANCON

MONTELIMAR

DIGNE LES BAINS

AIX EN PROVENCE NICE●

Acknowledgements

To Spence, the one man who heroically pulled me through the Alps and still puts up with my terrible banter when we're out cycling each weekend. Always the big cog.

To Jason, who now doubts me slightly less, but continues to destroy me on every hill climb we tackle together.

To Wes and Jonny, without doubt the two most entertaining people on the planet to watch a football match with.

To Ollie, Mollie and Don, for being my biggest supporters and the only people who believed this mad French expedition could be achieved.

To Jonny Ferry, for the use of your panniers, and to the security guard at Cherbourg Port who lent me your screwdriver so I could actually attach them to my bike.

To Andrew, Ruth and Pete, for being my in-house PR team and working your social media wizardry to keep everyone up to speed with my progress.

To my army of proofreaders, including all those mentioned above along with John, Rachel, Will and Dave. Your eagle eyes spotted far more mistakes than I'd want to admit.

To Cath and Fran, for your kindness over the years and for all the hours you put in to motivate people, young and old, to unleash their creative potential.

To Stephen Nolan and Denis McNeill, two genuinely gifted broadcasters, for your interest and unwavering support while I was out on the road.

To each person who donated during the trip and helped raise well over £3,500 for Street Soccer NI's work with less privileged people here in Northern Ireland.

To my B&B hosts in France: Eliane and Jean-Yves (who were much more generous and accommodating than I make them seem in this book), Sylvie, Ana-Livia and Antoine, Abdel and Sarah, Bertrand, Christian, Nathalie and Olivier, Cyril, Claire, Dylan and Laurene. All fantastic people, all easily contactable on Airbnb, and all 100% worth a visit.

To the Amalgamation of NI Supporters Clubs: the work you've done to transform the experience of following Northern Ireland over the last 20 years has been immense and should never be understated.

To our twenty-three gladiators who will go down in the history books: Michael, Conor Mac, Wee Shane, G-Mac, Jonny, Bairdy, Niall, Davo, Griggsy, Laffs, Conor the Postman, Roy, Corry, Stuarty, Luke, Ollie, Paddy, Aaron, Wardy, Craig, Big Josh, Lee and Alan. Never underestimate how much the summer of 2016 meant to us all, and how much of a part each one of you played.

And finally, to Michael O'Neill. The architect of dreams. Without your meticulous preparation and inspirational man-management, we would still be wallowing in international obscurity. We're no longer a laughing stock. You've built a team that's united a country. You gave us fans the opportunity to go to France – an experience we'll never forget. Without you, my bike would have sat gathering dust in the shed at home. Keep on working your magic. We're all right behind you.

Printed in Great Britain
by Amazon